STARTUP

THIRTY-SIX LESSONS
FROM COMPANY
FOUNDERS & CEOS

STARTUP

THIRTY-SIX LESSONS FROM COMPANY FOUNDERS & CEOS

TIM JACKSON

THE KILDARE PRESS

To E, whom I now follow everywhere

Rather like a habit
One can always break
And yet
I've grown accustomed to the trace
Of something in the air
Accustomed to her face

— ALAN J. LERNER

Contents

Managing people 119

Fundraising 147

Board skills 181

Focusing on what's important 213

Time management 245

How to cut the cost of
trial and error

ONE RAINY AFTERNOON in 1995, twenty-five years before this book was published, I picked up the phone at my desk in London and dialed a number near Seattle.

When someone picked up, I explained that I wrote a weekly column about technology businesses for the *Financial Times* newspaper. I'd noticed their company had just started up, I said, and thought it would be interesting to write something about them. Could I speak to the founder, please?

There was a pause.

"Jeff," the guy on the phone yelled. "There's a call for you. Some guy in London. Wants to talk about Amazon."

I'M SURE THE column I wrote after that half-hour conversation with Jeff Bezos is in the FT's archive, but I haven't gone back to look at it. (There's a saying from the old days of British print journalism, when you learned about the world from physical paper: *Today's news wraps tomorrow's fish and chips.* Meaning once it's printed and out there, it's no longer of interest.)

But about that interview, I do remember at least this. As someone who loved brainstorming business ideas, I couldn't resist throwing one or two thoughts at Bezos after I'd asked him all the questions on my list. "Why don't you have a loyalty program?", I suggested helpfully.

"Simple," said Bezos. "If you think about it — all those points, all those rewards — loyalty programs are about privileging existing customers over new customers. I don't want to do that. For the next twenty years at least, what I want is new customers."

Bezos was true to his word. By 2020, Amazon had more than 200m customers — an astounding number for a physical business that ships physical things to people. The company had 1.1m people on its staff, which made Amazon the world's second largest private employer, and with another 500,000 hires in process, was set to overtake Walmart as number one. Oh, and he was also the richest person in the world.

Yet it's only in retrospect that Amazon looks like a sure-fire success. After its IPO, lots of expert equity-market analysts pointed out that the business had never made a profit, and forecast that it never would. *Amazon.bomb*, they called it.

That tension sums up how a startup differs from other kinds of small business. A startup is a small business with ambitions to become enormous and maybe global, not just to being the best bookstore in the neighbourhood. To get big, it has to disrupt — to do things differently from the existing businesses in its industry. To disrupt, it has to experiment, since first attempts to do things differently don't usually work. And to experiment, it has to be prepared to lose money for a while. To fund its losses, it needs to find funding from people who are willing to put capital into ventures that are most likely to fail completely, but have a small chance of bringing a huge return — venture-capital funds. Those are the ingredients of a startup: global ambition, disruption, experiment, losses, VC.

If those ingredients sound like a combustible mix, that's because they are. The very high failure rates among startups indicate how easy it is to misjudge the balance between the approaches needed to run a small company and to run a big one. If you've opened a neighbourhood bakery and your first hire, a part-time barista, asks to leave early tomorrow afternoon to help their mother get home from hospital, then telling them to put their absence request in writing to the HR department a month in advance isn't likely to make it easier for you to hire employee #2. And if you have 1.1m employees, like Jeff Bezos did in late 2020, you're not going to be able to run your company effectively if you let your staff interrupt whatever you're doing to take random international calls.

THERE ARE LOTS of good books on the very early stages of building a startup, and many of them focus on product. Rob Fitzpatrick's *The Mom Test* is a great guide for how to ask potential buyers about what you're building and get truthful, useful answers. Eric Reis's *The Lean Startup* offers a great structured product-development process — start, define, learn, experiment, leap, test, measure, pivot, batch, grow, adapt, innovate. Steve Blank's *Four Steps to the Epiphany* gives a great playbook for customer discovery, customer validation, customer creation and company building.

But making a startup into a success involves a lot more than just getting the product right. What about the company itself, and how to manage it? You might think that the people most likely to do it right would be managers with years of experience at companies of the size the startup aspires to be. But sadly, those people have a poor track record in startups: big-company types tend to be better at telling others what to do than getting stuff done themselves — all hat and no cattle, as they say in Texas. And they often also suffer from analysis paralysis: too busy adjusting the five-year plan to figure out how to stay alive for the next five months. The result is that you can fail in a startup because of too much managerial experience as well as too little. Much of the learning that successful startup founders do is via trial and error. That's why venture capitalists give preference to 'serial founders' — people who have already run one or more startups, and who look like they have learned the right mix of hustle and rigour. Those people have gone through a managerial process of trial and error — but with other people's money.

WHILE EDITING THIS book, I had a catch-up videocall with a successful CEO whom I hadn't caught up with for a year or two. Gordon (not his real name) has exactly the profile that venture capitalists love: he's persuasive, analytical, trilingual, and has an engineering degree from a top Ivy. He's also a serial founder: he did one startup that didn't work, but acquitted himself well enough to persuade investors to give him money for a second idea. And when we spoke, he'd been running that second startup for a couple of years. It had flown like a rocket at first, and he'd raised three financing rounds. Yet over the course of that half-hour, Gordon revealed some things that had gone wrong — first some problems with sales, then some deeper problems with the product itself. Because the company was growing so fast, it kept burning cash while the issues remained unresolved. "If we'd addressed those problems earlier," Gordon confided at one point, "we could have saved our investors $10m."

Always make new mistakes. That's the line that a leading tech investor I know has had in her email signature for years, and it's a powerful point. Startup founders shouldn't be trying to avoid making mistakes; if they did that, they'd never be able to start anything, since it's always less risky just to repeat something you've already done. But they should try avoid *repeating* the mistakes they've made previously. Despite his company's lost $10m, Gordon had actually followed the advice perfectly. For even if the mistakes that he and his cofounder made about sales and product were familiar to me, the mistakes were *new to them.*

I'VE SEEN TRIAL and error at work in startups from four different perspectives. First, as a CEO myself — a job I decided to try after writing one hundred-odd columns about other people's startups. *How hard could it be*, I thought. The answer turned out to be way harder than I imagined: I made every mistake described in this book, and plenty more. But I was also exceptionally lucky — the timing was fortuitous, the company hired some brilliant senior people who could fill in my gaps, and we were able to IPO the business on the Nasdaq. After an exceptionally bumpy ride as a public company, the business I started was sold seven years later for just under

$2bn.

My second perspective on running startups has come from working as a VC — first leading a team of ten at a $700m venture-capital fund, a job I started right after my company's IPO — and latterly running a seed fund where I've tried to apply the disciplines of big-ticket investing to early-stage investing. Walking Ventures' returns may be in the global top tenth of the VC industry, but we've still seen lots of companies fail.

A third perspective has come from sitting on startup boards. Most investors in startups get 'information rights' — but that often means a bland, upbeat and uninformative quarterly summary. It's the board members who get to see the monthly detail and discuss the business in detail with the CEO at meetings. Across twenty or more startup board seats, I've seen many ways in which the story plays out. Even though most founders and CEOs instinctively present an optimistic picture to their boards, it's hard for the numbers to lie over the long term. So patterns gradually become visible in the gap between what the management say and what they deliver.

My fourth and final perspective has come from coaching CEOs outside our investment portfolio. This has been a revelation. Startup founders and management know that every conversation they have with a VC is an 'investor-relations' conversation, meaning that if they reveal incompetence, that could at best make it harder to persuade the VC to give them more money, and at worst could cause them to be fired. Once you remove that dynamic — once you take out of the room the elephant of a 20% shareholding in the business, plus a load of legal rights that limit the CEO's room for manoeuvre — it's easier to have a far more open and helpful conversation.

IF THERE'S ONE thing I've learned above all from thousands of hours of conversations with CEOs, it's that there is no single best route to building a startup. That may sound so obvious as to be banal. But it's surprisingly common to read books about entrepreneurs who create successful businesses, and to come away from them with subconscious to-do lists. (I'm partly guilty of this myself: I wrote books about Intel and Virgin — two companies that could hardly be more different. But I never seriously considered what Virgin would have looked like if hard-driving, analytical, detail-obsessed Andy Grove had been in charge, or what Intel would have looked like if it had been run by charming, casual, hands-off Richard Branson.)

That said, I've observed that there are a set of disciplines that are common to many of the most successful startup founders. Those disciplines range in scale from the micro (like how to deal with an email quickly) to the medium (like how to organise your week effectively) to the macro (like how to execute a long-term plan over multiple years). And they cover yourself, the team of people who report to you, and the entire company. I've represented this as a three-by-three matrix, and this book is organised around the resulting nine groups of skills.

One good way to use this book would be to look at the nine sections in the table overleaf, and use the page references to jump to the sections where you could do with the most help.

Some of these skills are vitamins rather than painkillers:

	MACRO	MEDIUM	MICRO
PERSONAL	Focusing on what counts *page 213*	Working with board directors *page 181*	Time management *page 245*
TEAM	Hiring and firing at scale *page 33*	Cofounders and top team *page 3*	Managing people *page 119*
COMPANY	Culture *page 63*	Getting results *page 91*	Fundraising *page 147*

they're important for the long term, and your company will still be in business tomorrow even if you don't have them. Those are skills that it's most appropriate to work on right after a company has just raised a big funding round, when it has plenty of time to get things right. To borrow a metaphor from venture capitalist Ben Horowitz, that's when you are a 'peacetime CEO'.

In wartime — when your company's very survival is at risk, and you may have only three months or six months to solve the problem — it's important to identify the two or three things you *must* get right to stay in business, and to postpone or ignore everything else.

If you're a wartime CEO, then it could be helpful to look at "How to run a startup that's running out of cash" on page 172; "How to save your marriage from your startup" on page 259; "How to close a funding round" on page 163; and

"How to know when to give up" on page 235.

The word 'Lessons' in this book's title may seem an odd word to use in the context of startup founders. They tend to be so smart and so individualistic that it's hard to imagine them sitting at a desk, copying things down written by the teacher on the blackboard. That's why these are lessons *from*, not for, startup CEOs. I'm reporting here things that I've learned — from CEOs that I've coached, invested in, served as a board director, or merely met while they were fundraising. In one sense, being a coach is like acting as a clearing-house: when someone I'm working with is stumped by a problem, often the most helpful thing I can do is point to how others have dealt with similar situations.

That said, I've interpreted the 'CEOs' in the title liberally enough to include myself. Some of the things I found useful both when running a company and now can be found at "How one big thing can lengthen your attention span" on page 214, "How to keep a good to-do list" on page 246, and "How batching and stacking can fix your time management" on page 252. Those chapters will give you some tools that can be used more generally to work effectively.

Whichever way you use this book, I'd like to know. What worked for you? What didn't? What could be improved? Please email me at tim@startup-book.net.

COFOUNDERS AND THE TOP TEAM

How many CEOs a startup needs

WHAT DO THE following companies have in common: Oracle, Chipotle, Whole Foods, Deutsche Bank, Salesforce and Warby Parker? They've all, at one point or another, had two CEOs at the same time.

This isn't a popular choice, to put it mildly. When Larry Ellison appointed two people to succeed him at Oracle in 2014, Fortune reported that only 22 of the 500 biggest companies had ever had co-CEOs in the last 25 years. It's like Charles Dickens's line in his novel Nicholas Nickleby, where he introduces a villain called Wackford Squeers with the words: "He had but one eye, and the popular prejudice runs in favour of two."

Except on the CEO front, the popular prejudice is clearly the other way round: one rather than two. What's the lesson here for startups and their investors?

LET ME BE frank: I don't think public companies are a good guide to solving this question for early-stage, fast-growing businesses backed by venture capital. That's because the real story of why big companies choose an unconventional solution to the CEO question is usually different from the happy fluff of the press releases. It's often the outcome of some vicious internal politicking, followed by an attempt at a peaceful solution — an armistice that lasts only a year or two, rather than a long-lasting peace treaty.

Here are the most common realities inside the boardroom that get companies into a two-CEO situation.

Reining in the emperor. Particularly in big public companies with an entrepreneurial founder with great energy and charisma, it's common for CEOs to go stale or to start believing their own PR. This can lead to bad decisions, which then alerts the board and shareholders that something needs to be done. They try to rein in the emperor, but the emperor resists. The board tries to promote him (it usually is a him, sadly) to chair and let someone else be the CEO. Then, when he resists again, it chooses the co-CEO solution as the second-best to settle for.

Board dysfunction. You've heard the line that a camel is a horse designed by a committee. Well, the board is a committee and its number-one job, many would say, is to appoint the next CEO. When boards are not just ineffective but also divided into factions, the result is sometimes that they can't agree. Co-CEOs are the least bad alternative to leaving the company without leadership at all. Either candidate might have done a good job, but their supporters didn't want to compromise.

The anti-Solomon solution. In the Hebrew Bible, King Solomon had to judge between two women each claiming that a baby was hers. He ordered the baby cut in half and split between the parties — at which point one woman burst into tears, and begged to have the baby given to the other. Solomon then revealed that he was just testing (ha-ha), and awarded

5

the child to the mother whose tears had proved her sincerity. The corporate equivalent is the reverse: two candidates who both believe strongly that they deserve the job. They conclude that half a CEO role is better than none ('and you never know, I may get to oust the other guy later on'). So they declare to the outside world how much they love each other, and share the job while privately sharpening their axes at home.

These are all terrible reasons for choosing a two-CEO solution. In all of the situations, the board will do their shareholders a favour by having the difficult conversations now, rather than some months down the road when harm will have been done to the business.

Few businesses would rationally make this choice. While giving one person the final decision isn't a great approach in politics (things didn't go well for the world with Hitler, Stalin and Mao in charge), sole executive leadership answers a number of big questions in business. Who will make the tie-breaking operating decisions from day to day? Who will present the business to outsiders and investors? Who will define the strategy and take responsibility for executing it?

This helps to explain why, in a mature business, a single CEO is the default answer that makes most sense to most companies. But for startups, there's often a chance to think about this from a blank slate rather than from the starting-point of replacing an existing incumbent in the job. And startups can have two reasons for choosing something other than a single CEO:

The soulmates. You have two people, usually founders, who have known and trusted each other for a long, long time.

They both have plenty of empathy. And they both believe two heads are better than one on most company decisions. The result is that they approach running a company as the business equivalent of pair-programming in software development. This situation is extraordinarily rare, but I know of at least two terrific tech companies that operate successfully like this. It's the best reason for having two CEOs in a business.

Too soon to tell. Early in a startup's history, the founders are untried. The candidate CEOs each have broad capabilities, and the roles aren't yet defined. The problem is to discern who's best for the role. It's a hard decision to make, and appointing two CEOs makes it much harder to choose one of them later: the inevitable demotion of the other one will be far more humiliating than never having had the crown in the first place.

That's why the zero-CEO solution can be a better choice at the earliest stage: it may may take a while for the founders to run the business for a while and to observe what they're each good at, what energises them, and what outsiders think of them. Once some time has passed, the transition to a single CEO can then be smoother. I saw this in one of my favourite startups, Tessian, which had three talented founders, each with a high degree of trust and empathy. Each of them could have been a fine CEO, but they decided mutually after a year or so that Tim Sadler should do the job.

Whichever situation your business is in — whether it already has a single CEO, doesn't have one yet, or has two — it's valuable to step back and think about whether the decision you've made about leadership is the right one. This is a hard thing to do because it's probably the one issue on which the founders have the least perspective. So a good approach is to try to look in as an outsider would. Here it can help to discuss the issue with board members and investors, and also a trusted external supporter such as a coach.

David Brown of Techstars, tellingly, has been in business with David Cohen for more than two decades, with each of them being CEO in different businesses, but has concluded firmly that the right answer to the how-many-CEOs question is one. He suggests asking four questions:

1. *Who thrives on the business issues and defers to the co-founder on the technical issues?*

2. *Who is tapped for media interviews, or leads investor pitches?*

3. *Who deals with contracts, negotiations and partnerships?*

4. *Who is perceived by others as the person in charge based on personality, attitude and assertiveness?*

I like the phrasing here. #1 avoids a judgment on skills, but focuses on what gives the founders energy (thriving) and the fact that a good CEO will defer to a cofounder on product. The reference to "tapped" in #2 clarifies that it's not the person who pushes hardest to get the speaking gig; it's the one outsiders respond best to. #3 correlates neatly with the bias towards action. And #4 acknowledges the reality that yes, assertiveness is part of the toolkit of a CEO: if you're always politely putting your hand up and waiting to be asked to speak, that doesn't just affect your standing inside your own company; it may also affect your ability to advocate for your company in the outside world.

But David's questions aren't a panacea, especially when the incumbent CEO doesn't agree with others about the answers.

How to choose a CEO

So how should a company which temporarily has either zero or two CEOs, or one facing challenges, figure out who to give the job to? Russell Reynolds, a big search firm, suggests that good CEOs combine nine qualities in three buckets:

Forward-thinking: plans ahead and is prepared for the future

Intrepid: Calculated risk taking (takes risks, but not carelessly); *Bias to thoughtful action* (is biased towards execution, but not impulsive); *Optimistic* (actively and optimistically pursues new opportunities); *Constructively tough-minded* (perseveres and is thick-skinned, but not insensitive)

Team building: Efficient reader of people (seeks different perspectives but doesn't overanalyze); *Measured emotion* (displays intensity but also control); *Pragmatically inclusive* (involves others, but also decides independently); *Willing to trust* (is comfortable with a range of people, but not credulous)

Using data from its personality testing of lots of senior managers, the firm reports that CEOs have these nine skills in much larger dollops than other execs. The biggest differentiators arc risk-taking, and trust.

9

The focus on risk-taking versus trust could be a consequence of where the research was done — among the client base of a big search firm. In corporate life, risk-taking is often in short supply in the cushy armchairs of the executive suite, but everyone has platoons of reports and therefore learned years ago how to trust them. In startups, by contrast, I'd expect the opposite: risk-taking is a quality common among founders, so a less useful way to pick the CEO, while the need for startup founders to do lots of stuff themselves at the start makes skilful delegation a scarcer commodity.

In boards and investments as well as coaching CEOs, I've observed that startups need more of a bias towards action than big companies — which means that in the bullet points above, the best candidate will have significantly more weight on the bits before rather than after the 'but' in each phrase.

Despite those cautions, the Russell Reynolds framework can be a useful tool for founders and investors. A good approach is to put the criteria in rows, and score the candidates, including the incumbent, from 0 to 5 on each of them, and then compare the totals.

WHAT IF YOU'RE the CEO, and you've gone through this exercise, either privately or with your co-founders, board or stakeholders, and the process has concluded that you're not the strongest candidate?

Well, congratulations. You're displaying an insight that most people don't have. Your insight can help you see that you have two roles in your company: as an employee, where you happen to be CEO, and where you provide services and get paid a salary and maybe bonuses and stock options in return. But you're also a shareholder, where you own a chunk of the business. That chunk is probably a large chunk of your total net worth, and will be worth a lot more if the business does well.

And that's the key point: if the business does well. As employee, you're the fiduciary custodian of this investment — not only for the other shareholders, but also for yourself. Obviously you want to hang on to your job; nobody likes to get fired. But if a point comes where, with your shareholder hat on, you conclude that your long-term investment in this company will do better if you replace that employee (ie yourself), then that's the time to do it.

It's also worth pausing to consider the consequences. The standard equity terms in VC-backed companies include 'reverse vesting', where the founders have to give back (or to be more precise, convert into a worthless 'deferred' class), a proportion of their shares depending on how long they've stayed since the investment. This is understandable, since almost no investors want to buy a business without leadership, and the company is worth much less if the founders leave. But standard terms also include 'good leaver' clauses that allow founders under the right circumstances to leave and take their equity with them. So a founder who's making heavy weather of being CEO may be a good leaver. That means he or she can continue to benefit from the upside, while going off and starting something else or taking a job that's more congenial.

FOR EVERY COMPANY where the first CEO was replaced too early, there are probably ten where the CEO was replaced too late — usually after considerable destruction of shareholder value. Many VCs, although they talk the talk about founders' professional development, privately take the view that 25% of them can make it, in the sense of continuing to do the job effectively all the way to exit or IPO. The 75% that can't will simply have to be replaced.

As a coach, I've seen many times that the investors' decision isn't a binary one between 'leave the CEO to get on with it' or 'replace them'. With help, half of the CEOs that might otherwise fall or be thrown by the wayside *can* acquire the skills needed to run their companies at 10x and 100x the size, and that's what this book is about.

But there are some founders who, even with coaching, don't make great CEOs after their companies mature to a certain point. For those founders, handing over to someone with more relevant skills can be the right thing. If that's you, then remember this: there will always be other startups, and the lessons you've learned from this company can be deployed again and again. And a founder who makes an indifferent CEO the first time can make a great CEO the next time.

How not to break up
with your cofounder

THE SINGLE BIGGEST reason why startups fail is that the founders fall out with each other. Yet even though venture capitalists are in the business of trying to distinguish companies that are going to succeed from those that are going to fail, it's near-impossible for them to learn much about how well the founders work together before they've invested. That's because when it comes to securing investments, wise founders will try to paint a picture of marital harmony. After all, letting the cracks show in the pitch meeting is a great way to attract nobody.

Even after the investment has closed, VCs have to recognise that co-founders are never going to be fully frank about their relationships — until the strains get serious. And when a VC gets the call, it's likely too late to fix.

But if you're a founder, you have a vested interest in the truth, so you're in a far better position to assess the strength of the relationships and the likelihood that you'll stay together. After seeing plenty of companies from the vantage point of an investor or board member, I've done some thinking about the sources of co-founder breakup. Although there isn't enough data to be statistically robust, I've observed that five factors are important in determining how long founders will stay together.

1. Advance planning and negotiation

Dashed expectations often cause founders to fall out. To avoid this, be honest. Have a frank, detailed discussion about everything that matters: how you like to work, how long you want to stay with the company, what jobs you'll do, that sort of thing.

Unfortunately, if you're already eighteen months into a startup, and you've realised that you and your co-founder have big differences on these points that are putting pressure on your relationship, then it's too late — and you can do no more than learn the lesson for next time. But when you're at the planning stage of a startup, it makes sense to discuss these (and other) things in detail, and commit what you've agreed to paper.

A written co-founder agreement (of which there are plenty of free templates out there) can help to get the differences on the table. Interestingly, I've observed that when two founders start a company together but have unequal stakes, that often reflects an honest and detailed conversation about who's contributing what, which resulted in a consensus. Equal splits are easier to agree, but can more often reflect a wish to delay confrontation.

2. Well-matched lifestyles

Since you typically spend more waking hours a week with your co-founder than with your lover, it stands to reason that if they have personal habits that drive you crazy, then it's going to be hard for the relationship to survive for long. But it's not so much about personal hygiene or taste in music; more about whether the contexts of the founders' lives are similar. It matters whether you have similar energy levels and outside personal commitments, whether one of you has health issues, a side project, even a longer commute. I've seen companies succeed where there are big differences here, but founders have to work harder to compensate.

3. A shared sense of fairness about the stakes and responsibilities

Someone's eventually going to ask: is the deal fair? That is, is each founder putting in time and effort commensurate with their stake in the business, and are they making proportionate contributions to the success of the company? There's nothing as lonely (or frustrating) as the feeling that you're the person pushing the car through the mud while your co-founders relax in the passenger seat — especially if you also feel you're not being fairly rewarded.

4. The present state of the relationship

Close relationships are resilient to turbulence. That's why VCs often prefer co-founders who shared rooms at university or who worked together for three years in a previous company to those who met each other at a hackathon two weeks ago.

But it's not just about history; it's also about how well the founders think they work together today: whether they like each other, chat over coffee or meals, or socialise together outside work. Again, there are plenty of successful companies whose founders leave their work relationships at the office and do their own thing at weekends. But other things being equal, deeper friendships between co-founders are likely to correlate with longevity.

5. Transparency between founders

As in a marriage, you're likely to stay together longer if you can discuss the issues in the relationship. So it matters if you can give each other candid feedback, if you talk freely about the state of the business, if you think responsibilities are allocated fairly between you — and if you've had conflicts in the past that you have successfully overcome.

You might think that if your business is going well, you don't need to worry about these things. The paradox is that success with the product and the plan can often mask failure with the people — not surprisingly, since if it looks as though the founders' shares in the company are going to be invaluable, there's more at stake, and more reason to stay. So if your business is on track for a billion-dollar exit but you have a recurrent worry that your co-founder hates you, you may be right. And you should do something about it *before* you file for the IPO.

It's often when the business runs into trouble that co-founder strains often become visible to investors. That's because without the gravitational pull of a giant pile of money, at least one person has reached the point of wondering whether walking away and doing something else could look like a better option.

IF YOU'RE WANTING to make sure your relationship with your co-founder is as good as it can be, then the factors I've listed above each give rise to an obvious list of action points. But beyond these specifics, it's worth remembering that there are three general ways in which co-founder tensions usually get resolved.

First is *renegotiation*. If I've got a gig on the side and want to get home in time for kids' dinner, then even a modest real-location of equity in the company may be enough to defuse the resentment and make everyone happy. The renegotiation won't be easy, because it requires honesty on both sides about what's really happening, plus a willingness to see things from the other person's point of view — but with help, it's achievable.

Second is *personal change*. If your co-founder is always at her desk by seven, inbox at zero, while you are still yawning into your cappuccino at eleven and not quite ready to start work, that's a source of tension. Again, an honest conversation may have different outcomes: you may decide you need to show more commitment in order to stay on as co-founder, or she may learn that actually, you're extremely productive and she shouldn't be clock-watching.

Third is *exit*. Even if it sounds like a nuclear option, it need not be, if handled properly. Plenty of strong founders like to work in small, friendly teams, but then find themselves out of their depth once they no longer know everyone they've hired. When the company grows beyond the skills of one of its found-ers, it's right to have an honest discussion. Again, the surpris-ing outcome is that a reasonable deal can often be reached on vested and unvested equity, and the departing founder is free to move on to their next gig. Which means a shorter, sweeter, separation than if the underlying issues are left to fester.

Sometimes it's helpful to have a third party moderate a discussion between founders about how it's going, and that's something I commonly do with CEOs when I'm acting as a coach. (Sadly, founders rarely tell their VCs about the issues until it's too late to fix.)

How to pick the right
people at the right stage

ONE OF THE thousands of mistakes I made in my first serious startup was to lose three of my first four hires. One of those was the head of marketing — let's call her Michaela.

Michaela had a stellar CV. She'd been to a top university. She had a decade of experience in the industry. And she'd worked for two of the top agencies in the world. She was way out of our league, and so expensive that the only way we could bring her on was to pay half her current salary and to give her a huge slug of stock options to outweigh the loss of the other half.

Yet a couple of months after Michaela joined, things weren't going well. We had a new strategy, but no new marketing projects and no new customers. Meanwhile, Michaela had had second thoughts about the half-equity deal she'd done. Within a few weeks, she was out of the door. (It was a decision she probably regretted, since the equity she left behind was later worth $10m.)

But Michaela wasn't the biggest hiring mistake we made. When it came time to take the company public, I felt we needed a CEO who knew how to talk to Wall Street. So we recruited an authoritative, impressive guy who gave me a strong feeling when I met him that the boss had just walked in the room (even though the boss was in fact still me).

He declared his ambition was to 'professionalise' the business. In this, he fulfilled all our hopes. Wall Street was impressed. We were able to IPO the business on the NASDAQ. And within a year, we'd acquired our biggest competitor for $1bn.

There had been changes inside, too. The senior people started flying business class rather than economy. The company moved from a cheap and grungy warehouse to a glinting glass and metal tower. And the new boss's BMW sports car, paid for by us shareholders, had its own reserved parking space in front of the entrance, so people practically had to clamber over it to get into the door.

"I think it's a great motivator," he told me at the time. "People know that if they work hard, they too can have a car like mine."

A few years later, the new CEO had declared victory and moved on to another job (with his car). But behind the façade, things weren't so great. The company had burned through 75% of the IPO proceeds, the capital markets were firmly shut to new fundraising, and the stock price had fallen by 99%.

THESE INCIDENTS RAISE three of the hardest questions facing startup founders. One is when to hire senior people (see page 26); another is how to avoid a train wreck after they join (see page 26). But perhaps the most important is how to pick the right people appropriate for the stage your business has reached. In thinking about this, I've learned a little from my own mistakes, a bit more from the companies we've invested in at Walking Ventures, but most of all from discussions with the CEOs I've coached.

The bigger issues usually boil down to two things: executing versus managing, and innovating versus scaling.

The executing-managing axis

When you start your own company, there are lots of things you have to do yourself — from buying and plugging in your own computer to (famously, at Amazon) building your own desk out of a cheap door. The result is that founders tend to become polymaths, and to have a bias not just to action but also to doing stuff for themselves.

As the company grows, the way to get things done starts to change from doing things yourself to getting other people to do them —and that means that the success of people at the top of the business is defined most by how effectively they find, recruit, organise and motivate others.

The innovating-scaling axis

Early on in the history of a business, the most important mission is to find product-market fit — to build something that people actually want to buy and are willing to pay for. Figuring out what will work is much, much harder than it looks: so much harder, in fact, that the smartest people don't try to do it. Instead, they try to build something that's their best guess of what product will fit the market, and expect it to be wrong. And they devote their efforts to a rigorous process of creating, testing, measuring, making changes and going back to creating, knowing that if they work hard enough and go round the cycle long enough, they're maximising their chances of success. That is a process of innovating.

But companies need to do more than innovate; they also need to get bigger. So as soon as you have a product for your customers (unless it's something that is so automated that it can sell itself, support itself, and deal with its own billing and customer-service issues), you'll need other people to deliver the product at scale. Which implies that there are four kinds of people needed in a startup:

Innovator-managers: People who can both come up with great ideas and also plan and organise. That is: people who can start and lead businesses. Let's call them founders.

Innovator-executors: To build your product, you may need developers, graphic designers, marketeers, content writers. Let's call them specialists, since they typically have a short list of areas of expertise, but their job is to come up with great new ideas in those areas. They can perfectly easily be individual contributors (ICs); they don't need to run teams.

Scaler-executors: As your company gets bigger, the demands in each department or activity become too much for an individual. You need more than one customer-support person, more than one sales executive. Bringing in these people is the way to scale the business. Let's call them operators because their job is to operate a machine that's been built. It may get tweaked and improved, but for this week at least, there's a defined process you want them to follow.

Scaler-managers: So you've got a product, and you've got customers. And you've got a growing crew of operators that need someone to organise, motivate and direct them. That's the typical profile of the senior hires that VCs are so keen to see their startups bring in. (Let's call them executives, but note the irony of the word: executives aren't executors; they're managers.)

The mix between those people will define the culture of your company ten times more than the dress code or the office decor. If you draw out the two axes, the results look like a two-by-two matrix:

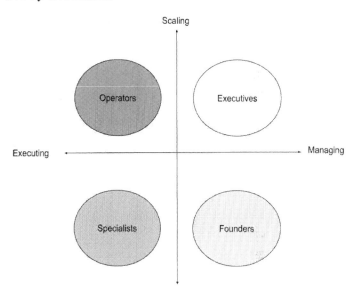

Jackson's Matrix for startup hiring

The y-axis goes from innovating at the bottom to scaling at the top. The x-axis goes from executing on the left to managing on the right.

A natural journey for a company is to travel clockwise

around the matrix starting at the bottom right. They start with founders only, who do everything themselves; then move left to hire some specialists as they get closer to product-market fit, who come up with new ideas but get stuff done by themselves. Next they move up to bring in operators as the business begins to scale, because they get things done using existing processes. And finally they move right to bring in executives to oversee the operators, because they manage teams of others and make the business grow.

In the real world, things aren't always so neat. Developers who write the code for a minimum viable product often turn into CTOs running a team of engineers. Or an inspirational sales advocate brings in the first few customers, and turns into the VP Sales who organises a repeatable sales process.

The difficulty in hiring in any particular area arises when the company is on the cusp of change. In sports, it's hard to be a player and a coach at the same time. In construction, it's hard to be a site manager and also a builder. And that's where many startups run into hiring problems.

One CEO I work with has hired a CTO who's great at running the team but doesn't write software. Six months in, he's improved the processes a lot, but apart from lots of refactoring, the company hasn't written a single line of new code. A lot of technical debt has been cleared, but customers are clamouring for new features and the board is getting impatient.

Another CEO I work with has hired a new (and very expensive) VP Sales. Three underperforming salespeople have been let go, and replaced with three much more senior sales people. The sales materials have been revamped, and a new CRM is in place. The probability-adjusted pipeline value report looks promising, but hasn't yet shown up in real revenue.

In both these cases, the CEO is uncomfortable — and the discomfort arises partly from mismatched expectations. The first CEO hoped that the new CTO would get the team to operate the tech side of the business better, but to keep innovating too — ie, to keep some of the tech team's effort under the line between specialist and operator. The second CEO expected the new VP sales to meet some clients and bring in some big deals too — to pull up their sleeves and be an operator.

THE MORAL FOR startups — and this is something to share with CEOs, if you're a VC, or with co-founders if you're a CEO — is that when you start a search for a new hire, try to mark the spot where the ideal candidate will appear on the matrix. If the founders and board can't agree on the answer, that's an indication that you need to discuss the company's needs for longer before finalising the job ad.

When you start seeing candidates, it's also a good idea to ask them where they'd place themselves on the matrix. If their answer is too far to the left of your target, then they're not senior enough. If it's too far to the right, they're not going to get their hands dirty enough. If it's too far up, they're not experimental enough, and if it's too far down then they're not expert enough in processes. But remember that these are your views, and you may not be right. It's worth comparing your view with the candidates, and inviting them to give you their view.

How to bring in a very senior person early on

"I'M SO EXCITED," said Edouard. "He's going to solve all my problems. He'll take over half the team, I won't have to manage him at all, and he's going to be like the co-founder I never had. He's going to transform the business."

That's a message I've heard several times from startup founders like Edouard. They got their company going by a combination of daring, intellect, and sheer grit. But now things have changed. Their first product has some traction, they've raised some money, and they're ready to get more professional. It's time to hire in someone senior from the industry, they conclude, who can help turn this into a serious business.

This impulse is valuable — in fact, investors ought to applaud when they hear it. Most founder-CEOs are comfortable having a crew of junior people. They don't actually want anyone in the company cleverer or more experienced than them. Only a minority are humble (and self-aware) enough to risk senior hires. The team at Notion, a top London VC firm, have collected data showing that companies that reach the mythical $1bn 'unicorn' valuation tend to add 3–4 new senior people in the year after their first venture round, while those not destined to be unicorns don't add any. The result is that a year after Series A, the proto-unicorns have 77% more years of management experience than their lesser peers.

But for founders like Edouard, bringing in a senior outside person with industry experience is a risk, because it raises very different issues from normal hiring. It's a risk not just that the hire won't turn out to be successful, but that it'll be a train-wreck: painful, damaging, expensive, and often sadly foreseeable some way up the track.

IT CAN TAKE a long time for founder-CEOs to admit to themselves, let alone to their boards, that the impressive new hire hasn't worked out. Partly this is because of the endowment effect (the phenomenon in behavioural economics that we value things more highly when we already own them). Partly it's sunk cost of a senior hire: much more time, effort and money than a junior. And finally, senior hires are more demanding and high-maintenance, and more skilful at managing upwards to an inexperienced CEO.

So what's the best way to avoid the train-wreck? After observing lots of these situations as an investor and a coach, I've identified three things that contribute to success at each stage of the process: before hiring, during negotiations, after they've started, and once they are up to speed.

Before hiring: make sure you are ready

Your company needs to be at the right point to get value from a senior hire. For instance, you need to have a sellable product before a talented but pricey VP Sales can turn it into revenue.

You'll need the right infrastructure to support them. People from large, traditional businesses have lots of support on hand: three interns to work on this project, a conference room for 1pm with sandwiches for six, an assistant to manage their diary and protect their office door from invaders. You can't offer these. But you need to be sure you can provide what they need to be happy and functional.

You will need to be ready for specialisation. As Andrew Chen wisely points out, the best early-stage hires at start-ups are often T-shaped people: deep in one area, but with a broad range of competences. C-level hires work differently. Their years of experience have made them great at one thing, whether it's HR, running a large tech team, or business development. If you need someone to contribute across the board, hire a smart graduate.

During negotiations, establish that there's a good fit

To persuade an accomplished senior person with a track record in an established business to take a risk on your company, you need to demonstrate two things: that you've made real progress beyond the deck-and-a-dream stage, and that the potential opportunity is huge. This is also their chance to change their industry for all time, and to be known as the person who did it. Unless motivations like these are present, they're only here for the stock options — and they'll start returning calls from recruiters the minute things look bad.

Be aware of adverse selection risk. Senior jobs in big companies bring prestige, money and security. On a strict calculation of present value, those things are worth more than working much longer hours at an uncertain startup. So a chunk of the candidates for your C-level job will be applying not because they're enthused by your mission, but simply because their current career ain't going anywhere, or they're about to get fired. To weed them out, you'll need to be meticulous in how you screen, interview and check references.

Manage expectations on both sides. It often works well to have dinner with them and their spouse or partner, and start an honest discussion about the sacrifices involved in joining your business. On your side, you'll need to up your game as CEO. You'll have to banish any remaining tendency you have to micromanage, but be alert to skilful office politics, which can mask poor performance.

After they've started, have a structured process ready
The traditional six-month probationary period may be the worst way to see whether a new senior hire is working out. Bring that reflection forward! A good approach is to check progress — not regularly every month or two, but at increasing intervals. One CEO plans short reviews after a day, a week, after two more weeks, and after one more month.

It makes sense to separate knowledge from achievement — to have a plan for what you hope the new senior hire will know, and what they will have achieved, by each waypoint. The actions are likely to be targets you will already have thought of, like 'assess the skills of the tech team within two weeks', 'update our roadmap in a month', 'redesign our channel strategy in three months'. The knowledge is often more subtle. It can range from the banal (people's names, how to use our CRM) to the significant (the special needs of customers in our industries). It's a good idea to set targets matched to the waypoints together with the new exec. Since it will probably take them six months to become fully productive, the separate knowledge and achievement checks will help you tell early on whether things are heading in the right direction — and prompt you to do something about it if not.

Hold a premortem

Whatever was said during the hiring process, there's room for extra frankness once the contract has been signed and the person is aboard. You can share thoughts about what might go wrong in the relationship, and to come up with plans for solving problems before they emerge.

Ensure the relations are right once the're settled

Your job as the manager of this new hire isn't over once you have successfully helped them stay in the job for six months and start to work productively. If you're going to keep them, it will require continued monitoring — not just one-on-ones, which good managers do with all their reports, but also paying particular attention to the special issues facing someone who has taken a big salary cut or made a big lifestyle change.

A good C-level hire can often make a significant contribution to your company strategy. But although it may be tempting to treat someone fifteen years older than you as your mentor, confessor or shrink, it's not advisable. If they are any good, they are likely to receive inbound approaches from competitors or their old employer. Sharing every one of your personal insecurities may tempt them to accept one. And if you really can't resist, separate the two discussions: don't use the one-on-ones in which you manage their performance as advisory sessions on company strategy or on your own personal growth.

Use your board as a reality check. If you have venture-capital investors, they are likely to have seen senior people join startups several times before. It can be helpful if one or more of your board members chats periodically with the new hire, to give you a candid assessment of how things are going. Of course, this requires confidence on your part: the paranoid founder will be terrified that the new hire will reveal to the investors that the company is run by an impostor.

To sum up: that first C-level hire is different from all your other hires. But you can significantly increase the chance that it will work out. And in recruitment fees, lost opportunities, strategic turmoil and frayed relationships, the saving to your company can be immense.

HIRING AND FIRING AT SCALE

How to run a good hiring process

"THE PRESSURE IS killing me," said Pablo. "My forecast said I'd bring in nine new people in the next six months, and the board keeps asking why headcount is way under forecast. Yet even with hiring taking up half my time, I'm not getting great candidates. I don't dare admit it to my VC investor, but I hired a couple of the people out of desperation — and now I may need to fire one of them. He was simply the wrong choice."

Pablo, one of the CEOs I coach, felt ashamed that he was doing a bad job on hiring — and he's not alone. A surprisingly high percentage of company founders raise money and then run into trouble when they need to bring in more people quickly without sacrificing quality.

Yet there are things you can do to get better at hiring. Through the investments in our portfolio and the boards I've sat on, I've observed ten things that companies who do this well have in common. Here's the list.

1. *Get the job specification right.* This means having a super-clear understanding of activities, qualities and objectives: what the person you want to hire will be doing, what skills and characteristics they need to have, and what you'll expect them to achieve in their first 90 days. Whoever the new hire will report to needs to decide these things, and write

them down. Start by deciding what needs to be done rather than who needs to be hired. When you run short of capacity in one part of your business, that can often be an opportunity to automate the boring bits, not hire more bodies.

2. *Get candidates from the right channels.* Most companies find that their best hires come via recommendation. To fully benefit from the networks of your team members, you need to do more than just offer them a cash bonus if someone they know gets hired. In his great book, *The Sales Acceleration Formula*, Mark Roberge suggests you forewarn people a few days before your next meeting with them that you're going to ask them to suggest a couple of candidates, so they can come prepared. Outbound matters too, since the best new people are likely to be doing well in their existing job and not looking for a new one. So identify sectors, companies and job titles where the dream candidate might come from. Then reach out to them via LinkedIn, professional networks or email. Job ads tend to produce lower-quality candidates, and in some circumstances contingent recruiters produce the lowest of all.

3. *Describe the job attractively.* Whether you're advertising or not, you need to be able to pitch the company and the job to candidates. Look at the dry description of responsibilities and requirements. Then repackage it, starting first with the reasons why your company is exciting and it would be a great move to work for you. Be thoughtful — and then minimalist — about required skills or experiences (is five years' prior experience as a content marketer truly necessary?). Every extra item on the list reduces your available pool.

4. *Write down your hiring process.* Structure the hiring process like a sales funnel, showing the different stages you want to take candidates through, the criteria you'll use to decide whether they progress to the next stage, and the percentage you guess will convert. This will help you avoid unnecessary effort by designing a process to filter out early on the people you can't hire. Also, don't ask for general cover letters: have candidates complete a structured form with specific questions covering the skills you're searching for. And before you bring them into the office for hour-long interviews with multiple team members, define some criteria for a short-list, and use 15-minute screening calls (video or phone) to identify your five favourites.

5. *Automate where you can.* Many parts of the hiring process, including scheduling screening calls, testing skills and personality, can be sped up 10x or 100x with automation. Some applicant tracking systems (ATSs) already include some of these features. You can hack others by hooking up tools like Zapier or IfThisThenThat to Trello, spreadsheets and email. It may not seem a priority to you to acknowledge job applications, keep your candidates updated on the process, and send polite and timely refusals. But it matters to *them.* One way to think about it: if you get 100 applicants for a job, then the way you treat the 99 people you don't hire will affect your reputation far more than the way you treat the one person you do hire.

6. *Use standard questions.* Put together a list of questions that will help you test for the skills and capacities you're

looking for, and ask every candidate exactly those questions. This makes better use of interview time, helps you compare like with like, and also improves consistency between multiple interviewers if you're sharing the burden. Try to include challenge questions (where you're pushing candidates to be fully honest about their past work experiences), insight questions (where you want to know what they learned and how they analyse) and scenarios (where they're revealing how they did or would react to specific work problems). Keep structured notes on their answers.

7. *Use quantified scores.* Many hiring managers make up their minds about candidates in the first few minutes. But you get better results by deciding a set of criteria beforehand, and then scoring each candidate against each time. You may end up with a result that doesn't accord with your gut. That's fine; comparing the candidate scored highest by your skills sheet against the one you instinctively want to hire can help you clarify whether you've changed your mind about which characteristics matter most or how each person rates on each skill.

8. *Get multiple people to decide.* If your company is big enough, you get a huge dividend from having multiple people take part in this process and the final decision. Google's research, as reported in *Work Rules!* by its 'people operations' chief Laszlo Bock, suggests you don't get much benefit from any interviewers beyond four — which is a useful tip to help you limit the burden you place on your team.

9. *Be realistic about the time and resource involved.*

Even with good processes, many startup founders underestimate both the number of candidates they'll need to make a great hire, and the time it will take. A good rule of thumb for each position filled is that the interviewing time alone will be 25 hours: five hours for screening interviews (say 20 candidates times 15 minutes) — plus ten hours for shortlist interviews (say five candidates times 30 minutes times four interviewers), plus ten hours (two hours times five candidates) for one interviewer to take a detailed and in-depth biography of the shortlisted candidates. And that's not including drafting the job spec, scheduling interviews or communicating with candidates. If that seems a lot, consider that a retained search firm recruiting for a senior job would charge a fee of $80,000 or more, and expect to devote 250 person-hours' effort to that single hire.

10. *Use an internal recruiter where appropriate.* It helps to have one person who is accountable for making sure you have the right number of candidates moving through the funnel at the right speed, and that the process is being well run. That's why for many companies it makes sense to hire an internal recruiter (who could be a contractor or a temporary hire) to do these tasks. If you are hiring six or more people in the coming six months, then the cost of this will more than pay for itself in faster recruiting and better-quality people.

THE TEN ITEMS on this list may sound pricey and daunting. But if you make any reasonable guesses about the cost to your company, and the stress to you personally, of hiring the wrong people — wasted training time, wasted salaries, missed business opportunities — then a well-planned hiring process suddenly looks like a bargain.

How to get people to accept your job offers

ONE OF THE few consolations of running a startup during a recession or a bear market is that hiring gets easier: there are lots of good people looking for jobs. In good times, when VCs have sprayed money at startups left and right, it's inevitable that hiring the right people gets a little harder. Whatever the economic weather, it's worth knowing how to make your company attractive. Skilled founders think about how to make the whole hiring and onboarding process more friendly to candidates.

Asking the CEOs I coach what their secret sauce is. I've learned nine things, plus one thing to pay attention to after the candidate has accepted your offer and you think the hiring task is done.

1. *Make the process structured and transparent.* A surprising number of startups don't have a clear answer when you ask them to list the exact steps they expect candidates to go through before they hire them — whether it's CV review, screening call, onsite interview, aptitude test, reference checks, whatever. A simple, clearly defined process that you can explain in thirty seconds will start your relationship with

candidates off on the right foot — especially if your competitors' hiring practices are Kafkaesque.

2.   *Make the process fast.* Research shows that companies that respond to inbound inquiries within 15 minutes get a hugely higher hit rate than those that take 15 hours. Yet few CEOs apply the same sense of urgency to hiring. One founder told me he had a standing policy of getting two of his board members to interview all candidates for senior roles (good idea), but each interview typically took three weeks to organise (bad idea). Talented people are in demand: they're likely to get offers from other companies, and anything that slows your process has to be weighed against the risk that the best candidate will sign with one of your competitors.

3.   *Check your hiring process for flab.* It's often tempting to make your hiring as thorough as possible, without paying attention to the number of hoops you're asking candidates to jump through. If you make the process troublesome and annoying for people, then you're going to lose multiple ways. You'll get more dropouts in the funnel (and they'll mostly be the best people who don't have to take nonsense from you because more reasonable companies want them). An over-elaborate process may also increase your own costs: do you need really eight members of the team to interview each candidate? And the candidates who make their way through your obstacle course might not love your company as much by the end as they did at the start. Consistent with quality, try to think about making life a little easier for them.

4. *Be true to your brand and values during the hiring process.* It's amazing how many companies that declare the ambition to be open, communicative and warm to their employees are exactly the opposite when they deal with people who want to become their employees. That's why it's useful to check all your communication, both written and spoken, and ask yourself how friendly it is to candidates. That starts with the wording of job ads. But it also includes:

- How promptly you reply to them — if you wouldn't ignore a client's email for ten days, why would you do that to someone who might be your next star employee?
- How much respect you show for their time — do you arbitrarily order them to come to an interview on a specific date and time, or do you give them a calendar link that lets them see a number of slots and choose the one that works best for them?
- How you treat people you don't want to hire — since you'll likely reject 98% or more of all candidates, how will the tone and content of your rejection email make them describe your company to friends looking for jobs?

5. *Understand your candidates' needs.* When you're choosing between candidates, it's easy to forget that they're also choosing between jobs — not just in terms of salary, commute, responsibilities and so on, but also which job will contribute best to their longer-term hopes and life plans. You can ask candidates about their needs early in the process, and have a thoughtful argument for why joining your company is

going to meet those needs best. It's also good to ask candidates about their blockers: what they disliked about previous jobs, and what things might make working for you harder. A classic example is software engineers who don't like to start early in the day. If you have a star candidate who wants to work late into the evening but can't bear the morning rush hour, for instance, then be sure you know their preference and can work around it. Showing your flexibility also sends a signal about how nice you'll be to work with over the longer term.

6. *Expose shortlisted candidates to the team.* Some people want to make friends at work and build a chunk of their social life from the office. Others just want to get the job done and go home. But almost everyone wants to work with people who are polite, talented, honest, and who pull their weight. Being happy among colleagues is one of the factors that makes people stay in their jobs. You can use this to your advantage in the hiring process: in addition to having candidates interviewed by different people in the company, you can also arrange for them to meet employees informally over breakfast, lunch or drinks. The more the candidate feels you have a crew of great people that they'd love to work with, the closer they are to accepting your offer.

7. *Use tests to see if they'll like the job, as well as if they're good at it.* Many companies that are good at hiring have developed ways of trying out candidates on activities that they'll actually be doing once they join, in the form of tests, try-out days or selection weekends. But it's not only one way:

remember that the candidates are also evaluating you. You
don't want to mislead them — the only thing worse than not
persuading a great candidate to join is having them join, but
quit two weeks later when they realise what the job is really
like. It's worth thinking about how you can help them get a
taste of working for you early enough for them to tell whether
they're going to like it.

8. *Use stock options wisely.* The classic Silicon Valley
model of giving everyone stock options has lots of advan-
tages. The spring of 2019 was a particularly good time to
observe this, as the IPOs of Uber, Lyft, Airbnb and Pinterest
turned several thousand people in the city of San Francisco
into millionaires, with the New York Times reporting on the
scramble this created among real-estate agents, car dealers
and wealth advisors. If you're a company founder, it's easy to
take for granted the magic of stock options. But don't assume
that potential hires understand it too. It's your job to educate
them. Rather than just say "This job comes with options over
20,000 shares, which are currently worth 50 cents each,"
which they'll immediately multiply to get a figure of $10,000,
it's valuable to start with the mission (see page 73). then
explain your grand plan to change the world, and then go
on to show how valuable your company will be when it's
achieved. So if your company's value per share hits, say, $10
or $50, then the options aren't "worth" $10K. Instead, they're
a lottery ticket that could be worth $200,000 or $1m.

Obviously you remind new hires that you can't guarantee
the outcome. But you can make it clear, with evidence, why

it's plausible, and you can make them feel that they're a part-owner of the business too, and they'll benefit from its success. And you can also give the potential employee a calculation showing that due to the favourable tax treatment of stock options in many jurisdictions, you'd have to earn a lot more than $200,000 in salary to get the same benefit as the same amount in options.

9. *Make your job offer in the warmest possible way.* Sending someone an email to make a job offer can seem cold. Several CEOs I've worked with make a point of making the offer over phone or videocall, sending the written offer just beforehand and giving the candidate a chance to go through it line by line to ask questions about the details. Some will actually invite the candidate in for a meeting, perhaps a final interview or a lunch, and will then reveal the offer. This gives you a chance to show how enthusiastic you are about the person joining, and how bright a future you think they have inside your company.

SO THAT'S A list of things I've seen CEOs do to make their companies more attractive to job applicants.

But there's more. It's not unknown for candidates to accept your offer, give notice to their current employer, and then decide to join another company instead. Interestingly, it's a one-way risk: if you as the employer make a job offer and withdraw it, you're likely to be in hot water and liable for damages if the employee can show they've been harmed. (Look at the $100m lawsuit that banker Andrei Orcel launched against

Santander after it became clear he wouldn't, after all, be joining them as CEO.) By contrast, employees who renege on a contract with you will mostly get away with it. How do you stop them from being tempted?

10. *Aim to increase people's excitement after they've accepted your offer.* One way to think of it is that you're trying to reduce the risk of buyer's remorse in the employee's mind. Over the period when they're working their notice, you want their engagement and enthusiasm for working with you to increase. There are several ways to do that:

- Help them prepare before they join — whether it's researching the market, making a plan, or making relevant contacts
- Reassure them that they've made the right decision, both explicitly and implicitly; encourage them to update their LinkedIn and other social media to reflect their upcoming new job (this is valuable because it alerts all their contacts early on)
- Immediately start the discussion about what their first set of objectives should be, and what knowledge they should expect to acquire during their first week, month or quarter
- Invite them to company events, and shower them with company-branded merchandise, not only for themselves but also for their family
- Offer more chances to meet their new colleagues, whether it's dinners, offsites or company picnics.

DIFFERENT COMPANIES HAVE different approaches to how they treat candidates; take any one of these approaches, and there are good arguments against it. But a good exercise would be to look at your hiring and see how many of the points above you can confirm that you already do. If the number is six or fewer, and you're having trouble getting people to accept your job offers, then you've got a good list of things to try.

How to tell when you need more managers

BY ANYONE'S STANDARDS, all three of them were talented and successful CEOs. Pete had come from Goldman, via private equity. Helena had made great indie films. Gustavo had been a star commodities trader. They'd each started their own businesses, and raised a combined $20m from investors.

But one on one, all three revealed their own separate struggles. Pete talked about the trouble he was facing with staff turnover, and figuring out how his organisation should be structured. Helena had a tech problem: her lead developer was talented but temperamental. And Gustavo had brought in a superstar head of product, who turned out to be no improvement on his own efforts.

The obvious problem here was hiring mistakes. They're expensive in several ways:

- The raw salary of people who don't perform.
- The time required to recruit replacements.
- The opportunity missed in sales that fail to close if you have the wrong people in place.
- And above all, the grief — because the only thing more stressful in a small company than managing underperformers is having to fire them.

Beneath these apparent differences, the three founders were facing a common issue: setting up their company's first tier of management. Do it too late, and you find yourself as CEO with an overwhelming queue of people by your desk asking for input, help or approval. Do it too soon, and you risk having a prickly relationship with a senior hire.

Your first senior hire may have more experience in your industry than you have. They may send subtle signals that they don't think you know what you're doing. Or make unflattering comparisons between the rigorous approach of the big company where they used to work and the amateurism of your startup.

It's hard to forecast how big a company will be when it needs to start putting in its first layer of management. One view is that that one manager can look after no more than six reports — that's what Andy Grove, Intel's pioneering CEO, advised in his brilliant 1988 book *High Output Management*.

On that basis, employee number eight needs to be the first manager. Intel's own founders, interestingly, took an extreme approach: they were so confident that their business would get big fast that they hired people from the start who already had a track record of managing others.

If there are two or three co-founders with different areas of expertise, then you could get to a team of maybe 15 without needing any managers. In a service business (or one where some functions are done labour-intensively by large numbers of relatively junior people), you might reach 20 or 25 without managers. The right answer depends on your industry, your product and how you deliver it.

The key thing is to watch for the signs that your available management resource is being overwhelmed and it's time to hire another manager. Here are some questions you could ask yourself.

- Are you becoming a personal bottleneck on decisions? If your team members complain that they often have to wait for sign-off from you, it's time.
- How many of your team members did you barely talk to in the past week? If the number is above zero, there was no special reason like travel or sickness, and they don't have a manager to report to, it's time.
- Is your team inadequately supported? If you feel some of them aren't performing at their best, but you don't have time to sort out their issues, it's time.
- Also, look ahead: do you think you're going to need to hire six or more people in the coming six months? If so, you should be thinking now about who will manage them, and how. It's time.

ONCE THE TURNING-POINT has been reached, how do you ease the transition inside the business? In the course of working with dozens of CEOs, I've observed a number of approaches that can help.

Start to tilt your hiring criteria towards management skills. You're no longer just looking for people who are great at selling or writing code. Now you need people who also have the ability to lead other people doing the same thing. And you need to put in processes that will work when those people start to manage teams of their own. That means different job ads, different interview questions, different hiring approaches. But there are risks in hiring someone who expects to spend their time telling other people what to do. The sweet spot at Series A is often what the construction industry calls a 'working foreman' — someone who can coordinate plumbers, electricians and labourers, but isn't too proud to tile a bathroom themselves. (For more on this, see page 19.)

Start to prepare for a transition in your role. In your one-on-ones, you'll no longer just be asking how they're doing and supporting their projects. Now you'll be helping them manage the people beneath them. A good framework to use is SCRIM: you'll want to check regularly whether the people in their team are Suitable for the job; adequately Coached; Reliable; given the right Incentives; and Monitored by checking on the right stuff. (See page 92.)

Evaluate the role of culture in your hiring. It's a truism for companies to seek new joiners who fit the existing culture. But all founders make mistakes, and early hires are often among them. If you've made one or two hires that you're beginning to question, then giving them vetos over new recruits may perpetuate your problems. Ask whether you need to change the culture a bit; if so, you may need to be more centralised in your recruitment decisions.

Think carefully about underperformers. Are they doing badly because you're not giving them enough support? If so, then more effective coaching and monitoring could transform how they're doing. If the problem is that they need new people above them, then you'll need to discuss that to ensure they'll be happy to stay as an individual contributor. And if they're actually not up to the job, then it's humane as well as professional to give them clear feedback on their performance. Then set clear expectations and goals, and signal to them that if they can't deliver by a specified date, then you'll need to let them go. This gives them a chance to start looking for a job where they'll do well, which is much easier to do while still employed.

Learn to become more open. In many startups, the founder's expertise and competence are far greater than those of the people they hire. When they start hiring more senior people, that disparity disappears. So more and more, your reports will have better ideas than you. You'll spend more time putting problems in front of people, and less time showing them solutions.

Finally, remember that professional development is now part of your job description. Salaries, bonuses and stock options go only so far to make employees happy. To be truly fulfilled, people need not only autonomy and purpose, but also mastery — a feeling that they're acquiring skills that they didn't have before. Quite soon, people will be asking you about their 'career paths' (see page 85). Even now, you need to be able to articulate to every new and existing employee what expertise they can hope to build over the coming year, and what the company can do to help them achieve that.

IT'S NOT AN easy transition, so don't blame yourself if you haven't got it 100% right yet. But if you watch for the signs that you need to bring in more managers, and then start to change how you yourself work, then you're maximising the chances of success.

How to decide whether
to fire someone

"I'M WORRIED ABOUT Philippa, my chief marketing officer," said Artemis. "She's a lovely person, but we're just not getting the results. Our company has a high cost per lead and a long sales funnel. Our conversion rate will ultimately determine whether we have a profitable business over the long term. But Philippa just isn't fixing it. Something has to change. Maybe it should be who does the CMO job."

Five years ago, I was an active investor who brought with me the experience of running my own startup. I hadn't been a great CEO. I'd been very lucky, but made lots of mistakes. I knew that in my own company, I'd kept on several people who weren't right for their jobs long past the point when I should have let them go, and I wanted to save others from doing the same. So my reaction to Artemis's question then would have been immediate. I'd have passed on a piece of wisdom I learned from an investor in my own company: *if you think that maybe you should fire someone, then you probably should have done it three months ago.*

Many people think it's unkind to fire people, and of course hate doing it. So I'd have offered some good reasons to a CEO in a tight spot. I'd have reminded them that:

- Your job is to build a great business, and you can't do that with the wrong people
- You've promised your shareholders not to misuse the funding they've put into your company
- This is an ethical responsibility just like being kind to others
- Also, hiring is a perfect example of the cognitive distortion of the endowment effect: the effort we've put into finding and training people can make us irrationally unwilling to admit our mistake.

That was my take five years ago. Today, after making a lot more investments and coaching lots of CEOs, I've changed my mind. Rather than saying Artemis should immediately call the underperforming Philippa into her office, with security ready to escort her out of the building and IT ready cut off her logins, I believe she should ask five questions before deciding her next move. Three of those questions, I've learned, are more about you as CEO than about the person teetering on the brink of being told to go and find a new job.

TO START, REMEMBER that in some circumstances, the right thing to do is to fire someone immediately — like theft, fraud, and other criminal behaviour at work. In deciding whether the person's behaviour falls into this category, you'll want to verify the facts, understand the law, check their employment agreement, and consult your lawyers to ensure that you have the right to fire them. And you'll want to follow the right process. This may include a suspension and investigation rather than a dismissal on the spot. It may require giving a written warning if the behaviour isn't quite serious enough to count as a 'repudiatory breach' of their employment contract. Or it may mean terminating their contract immediately once the investigation results have come in, or if they're repeated a serious behaviour and have already been given one warning.

Luckily, that's not the situation with Artemis's CMO, Philippa, where we're talking about underperformance, not sexual harassment or faked expense claims.

Also, as companies grow, the decision to fire someone rests with a manager rather than with the founder or CEO alone. In some cases, the decision will be shared between different people. Regardless, here are five questions that it's valuable to ask.

1. *How are they failing?* Start by privately making a list of the things the employee is doing that they shouldn't be doing, and the things they're not doing that they should be doing. Once you have this in writing, you can compare the list with their employment contract, with their job specification, and with the ad you used to attract them in the first place. If the failings you've identified don't mesh with these documents, then your problem is with communication. You need to tell them clearly, with a follow-up in writing, what you want their responsibilities to be and how you'll judge their performance. (You'll also need to do the same for the rest of your employees as well, so you don't get into this situation again.)

Note that this could constitute a change to their contract. If you hired them to run marketing and now you want them to manage a team of twelve sales people, then their inability to take on that new set of responsibilities may not give you a contractual right to get rid of them.

In some countries, like France and Brazil, making a mistake about your right to change people's roles could be a very expensive breach of contract, since you'll owe them compensation if you get it wrong. In Britain (where employees don't get their full protections until they've been with you two years) or in the US (where it's common for companies to employ people 'at will', meaning they can fire them for any reason or no reason), you may not have litigation risk, but you still have moral exposure. Firing someone for failing to do something they never knew they were expected to do may be legal, but it's bad karma.

2. *Why are they failing?* Now you need to dig a little deeper. Add an extra column to your list of failures, and write Cause at the top. Then, for each of the failures you've identified on the list, try to pick a word that captures why the employee hasn't met your expectations. The issue behind each failure is likely to fall into one of the following buckets:

• *Consistency*: If they generally perform well, but the issue is that sometimes they don't, then the problem may be that they're not hitting their metrics. One week they make fifty sales calls, the next week they make three. That raises a question: are you clear what a reasonable target is, and have you communicated that? Often, an apparently under-performing employee can deliver a radical improvement once they know precisely what's expected of them — or, as that slightly unappealing phrase has it, 'what good looks like'.

• *Motivation*: If the employee shows up late and hung over every morning and looks glum in team meetings, but has their bag packed and their computer powered down the minute their working day ends, then maybe, just maybe, they're not passionately devoted to their job. It's your job to make sure the people who report to you are given adequate incentives. That could be salary, bonus or stock options. It could be a sense of belonging and being valued. Being given interesting work and enough freedom to do it. Feeling connected to the company's mission. If looking through that list, you see some areas where this person (and perhaps other employees) aren't being given the right incentives, then that's something you need to work on.

• *Execution*: Once an employee has the skills and support they need, then it's up to you as their manager to make it clear what they need to do to be reliable. For a developer, this could be documenting code or following a deployment process. For a sales person, following a process with prospects and keeping a CRM updated. For a senior manager, it could be holding regular one-on-ones with their reports and supporting them properly. It's your job to define what counts as reliability for your reports, and to hold them to it.

• Knowledge: Sometimes the employee doesn't actually know how to do the job properly. If you're not sure whether they know, then it's your job to find out: get them to talk you through some of their tasks, and observe how they carry them out. If you discover that they have no idea what process to follow, then whose fault is that? Every company has its own unique way of doing things. You can't blame someone for not following your process until they have been coached and shown what to do and if necessary how to do it.

• *Suitability*: It may be that you're doing everything you should be doing to support the employee, but they're just not cutting it and you don't see any evidence that they're likely to be a high performer any time soon. If you put most of the issues on the employee's failure list down to Suitability, that's an indication that it may have been a mistake to hire them in the first place. Time to move on to the next question.

3. *How clearly have you told them where they're failing?* Now you add another column to your list of the employee's failings, this one headed *Informed?* — because it's a key part of your job as CEO to make sure all your staff understand how well they're performing, and what's going well and what's going badly. The first place to look would be in the documents or other written records that are part of your performance review process. What, you don't have written performance reviews? Well, that's something you need to fix. It's often intimidating to be called in for a meeting with the boss, and easy to forget or misunderstand what you've been told. A well-run company gives employees written feedback on how they're doing. Even if you don't have a formal appraisal system, an email trail at the least would help to confirm that

you've alerted the employee to the problem. You can put a Yes next to each failing where you can clearly document that you informed them they weren't meeting expectations. If you can't document that you told them, then it's a No. The way to remedy the situation is to arrange a meeting with them, share the list, and explain that things aren't working out and that you want to remedy the situation before it gets too serious.

4. *How clearly have you told them how to put it right?* In a well-ordered company, nobody gets fired just for under-performance until they've had a period to put things right. It's much more specific than that: they get a set of written targets to achieve, a deadline, and a warning that if they don't succeed, then their future is in jeopardy. This is a 'performance improvement plan', and needs to be presented with consideration for their feelings. If they feel that the opportunity they're being given to fix things is fake, and their firing is inevitable, then the resulting stress can make them do worse, not better.

An effective boss will begin the conversation by pointing out what is going well and the areas where the employee is performing up to standard, and will also give the employee a chance to explain any context or circumstances that might explain the underperformance. You'll do your best to convey to the employee that you want the best for them, and that you care about them even though you're responsible to the company and its shareholders to make sure it has the right person in each job. This isn't easy. You can sound banal or insincere when you try it, especially if you don't have a solid history of ethical behaviour that shows it's true.

You'd be surprised, though, how many employees suddenly shape up once they're told in detail, unmistakably clearly, what the problem is and what they need to do to fix it.

5. *Have you helped them put it right?* All good CEOs try to hire the best people they can. But the most effective CEOs I've worked with go further than that: they try to make everyone on the crew be the best they can be in the job they're doing. That's what people remember, by the way: the boss who gave them the greatest opportunity to grow professionally during their career.

AT THE END of the day, after you've done your best to help them perform, it's your job to determine whether someone reporting to you is in fact suitable for the job. If they're not, then it's your duty to tell them so promptly in a humane way, and let them get on with finding another job while you find someone else to fill the role. So while your decision to fire someone should never be hasty, your obligation is straightforward. If the answer to all five of these questions is 'yes', it's time to do it.

BUILDING CULTURE

How to bridge the work-ethic gap

THERE ARE MANY things that CEOs find it hard to talk about with their investors and board members. After all, board members have a fiduciary responsibility to shareholders, including deciding whether the company's current CEO is the right person. So confessing failure, mistakes or incompetence to a board member can be risky. In a coaching session, by contrast, hiding problems makes no more sense than hiding your symptoms from a doctor.

But it's not just failure that CEOs can feel embarrassed to raise with their investors. Sometimes, the issue can seem — well, maybe just too small. That was the context behind a question I was asked twice in the same month: "How do I get my team to work harder?" As our discussions unfolded, something interesting became clear. This isn't a small question; it's a big one.

THE TWO CEOS that raised the issue are very different. One is female, the other male. One is technical, the other not. One works very long hours at the office; the other leaves at five, and works at home in the evenings. One has a significant other with a demanding job that leaves little time for fun; the other has a spouse and kids. But they both lead extremely successful companies — and their sense of restlessness with how the business is doing and their anxiety to move faster may explain why their companies are so successful. It's a bit like the old saying: If you want to get something done, ask a busy person to do it. By contrast, one of the least successful investments I've ever made was in the company whose founder talked most about work-life balance.

The anxiety of the CEO-in-a-hurry manifests itself in distress from seeing people:

• Rock up late for work, and spend lots of time chatting or drinking coffee, but then down tools as soon as their contractual working hours end, no matter what they're doing

• Failing to complete projects when they hit an obstacle, and instead waiting for their manager to tell them what to do next

• Leaving big problems unsolved, even when they're time-sensitive and harm the company

• Disengaging from challenges facing the business, and expecting others to think imaginatively about how to over-come them

Part of the problem is that startup founders, and especially founder-CEOs, are unusual people. They're harder-working than normal (though I've found that often, strategy consul-tants probably outclass them: lots of McKinsey alumni have told me that their first assignment as a BA, or business analyst, taught them that they could achieve far more than they ever imagined possible, partly just by working from early in the morning until late at night for days and weeks on end).

Also, good startup founders, like strategy consultants, know how to break down big problems into lots of constituent parts, which helps them resist procrastinating or being intimidated by a big challenge. Such founders often find it hard to see the weakness of lesser mortals.

Don't forget, though, that founders potentially stand to gain a great deal personally from their company's success. Every investor pitch about the 'billion-dollar exit' reinforces in their own minds why they should spare no effort in trying to make a success of this once-in-a-lifetime opportunity. Hired hands, by contrast, don't have nearly as much at stake. They're playing for $10 a point, not $10,000.

Even when the founders dole out generous quantities of stock options, and ensure that even employees who leave before fully vested can make a substantial amount from their contribution, the numbers are usually too small to be life-changing.

And there's also the 'endowment effect'. It applies in spades to startups: if you're the founder, you're likely to believe in its likely success much more than anyone else. You'll value each share more than any of your employees do.

So it's only reasonable that founder-CEOs should care more and work harder. That said, there's a wide range of commitment and diligence in the general non-founder population. For some, work is something that pays the rent but shouldn't encroach on their 'real' lives. A few, if they have a gap between tasks at work, will welcome the chance to do nothing. That's something you used to see in the days when supermarkets used stick-on price labels instead of barcodes: the checkout clerks were often happy just to chill out for a minute or two, escaping the monotony while someone else solved the problem by strolling up the aisle to get the product's price.

If you're running a startup, and your company is unprofitable but growing fast, it depends on you to keep raising new money. The trajectory towards break-even can be measured in months, but it can also be measured in effort. So if you compare two startups, one staffed with people who put in 25% more effort than the average person, and the other staffed with people who put in 25% less, the first will get 125/75, or 66%, more done than the second. And if the people in the first startup do an hour's more work a day than average, and those those in the second do an hour less, then the total effect (multiply by 10/8) is more than 2x. Even if the first startup pays 25% higher salaries and offers extra benefits worth 25% of salary, it will still end up a net 40% ahead. So when recruiting, it's valuable to screen for people who work hard.

That's not easy, though. People don't admit that they're lazy in job interviews — yet one clock-watching chatterer can have a big effect. If that person does the bare minimum and gets away with it, then the rest of the team will wonder whether they're fools for over-delivering.

But the solution can't lie only in hiring and firing. What else can you do to motivate your team to work harder? If you look across the business landscape, you can boil it down to five approaches, two of which I don't recommend to CEOs and three of which I've seen work well.

FIRST UP, THERE'S a whole raft of ways that technology has made it possible to monitor people at work (not only when they come and go, but what they do), and to block them from doing things you don't want. Some companies, for instance, have reported that firewalling Facebook immediately improved productivity. Others have reintroduced punch clocks for the digital age. Some have even borrowed the monitoring tools from remote-working marketplaces which snapshot workers' screens every fifteen minutes.

These tools may help to limit the ways in which your employees can skive off work. But they have side-effects and a troubling implication. The side-effects are to stop people doing things that are valuable for your business — how can someone manage your social media without accessing Facebook? — and from exercising their right to use their break or lunch as they choose. And the implication is that you care only about workers' physical presence and about the task they're performing. Some good, hardworking employees may not appreciate this lack of trust, and may quit as a result.

A second approach in the same spirit is to bribe people to work harder — and to bribe them using currency that they overvalue. A case in point is giving free take-out in the office to people who work late. Or giving people computers and phones that make it easier for them to work from home. Ten years ago, employees were easy to fool with techniques like this. Today, they're more cynical about such benefits: they can easily calculate exactly how much the free food works out at per hour as compensation for their time, and they're more alert to the risk that a piece of technology that extends their employer's incursion into their personal life is a handcuff, not a gift.

So it's wise to use these two techniques either not at all, or only with great caution. They can sometimes work: a smart CEO I met offered his team gym memberships that were paid for by the company only if they went eight times a month, and then instituted a time-clock in order to remove the 'unfairness' of employees goofing off work to catch up on gym visits. But these situations are few and far between.

SO WHAT CAN work, then? Three things seem to have proven their worth. One is to increase the team's alignment with the mission of the business: the 'why', as Simon Simek calls it. At first sight, it may be hard to get people excited about your company's mission if it's not obviously heroic like taking humanity to Mars, or replacing all the cows on the planet with lab-grown meat. But there are ways to get your team more engaged in what you're doing even, if you can't portray it as world-changing.

One way is to make sure everyone knows and fully understands the customer problem that your product or service solves. If they feel the customer's pain, they'll be driven to stop it. Another is to take the time to learn the inner motivations and ambitions of each team member — not the list they gave you when interviewed. That can often give you ways to match people's responsibilities with their preferences and their aims, so they can help the company achieve its goals while striving for their own.

A second approach that CEOs have found successful is to

recognise that all of us get satisfaction from mastering new skills. (I'm a personal example of this; I've made significant changes to the work I do roughly every two years through my entire career, precisely because learning to do something well feels more fun than repeating something you can do in your sleep.) If you manage people, you can help them identify things they want to learn, and courses or books where they can do so. In one-on-one meetings, you and other managers can explore people's processes, to stimulate ideas for how to do things better, faster or cheaper — and you can celebrate and praise the specifics of what they achieve.

Most broadly, you can ensure that everyone in the company understands that the job they could be doing a year or two from now could be bigger and more serious than today's. In a large, slow, mature business, that may be a hard claim to sustain. But in a startup that's growing fast, it's almost always true. If the sales team grows from four to twenty, the head of sales could become VP and the two best salespeople could lead teams of their own. The desire to learn more is one of the things that gets people up in the morning, and prompts them to try to do their job better.

THE THIRD AND final thing you can do to encourage your team to work harder is to give them more autonomy. "Hey, wait," said one CEO during a coaching session. "Isn't that the wrong way round — if I give them more freedom, won't they do less work, rather than more?"

Only if you leave the job half-done. A good example is Netflix's famed unlimited vacation policy. That's a way of giving workers a much higher degree of autonomy — especially in the US, where plenty of professionals take less than two weeks off a year, in contrast to the easy-going European habit of four or five weeks plus public holidays. And it's true: if your only way of measuring your employees' output is to count the hours they spend at the office, then when you stop counting they may spend fewer hours.

But measuring your team's hours doesn't measure whether they do anything useful in those hours. You may have heard the description of how to become a great writer attributed to Ernest Hemingway — 'the art of writing is the art of applying the seat of the pants to the seat of the chair'. But the line in fact came from a much less famous writer-activist called Mary Heaton Vorse. Hours of application alone may be necessary, and can make you Vorse. But they're not sufficient to make you Hemingway. And Netflix realises this: the reason for giving employees freedom to set their own vacation is that the company has figured out how to set objectives for everyone, and how to hold people to delivering on those objectives. So the message from the top is a simple one: if you achieve what we've agreed on, we don't care how long you spend on the beach.

There can be lots of little ways in which founders and managers can take away autonomy from employees. I heard a striking example from one CEO, whose VP of Growth, responsible for the entirety of sales and marketing, revealed that he thought two of the people in his sales team were underperforming, uncoachable and should have been replaced long ago. Yet when asked why they were still in his team, the VP replied simply that he thought firing them wasn't something the company would have wanted. That's a perfect example of lack of autonomy: despite his seniority, the VP didn't feel he had sufficient room for manoeuvre to make the right decisions.

What this means in practice is:

• Clarify the areas in which people have the freedom to decide how to operate

• Ensure they know that you'll challenge them to explain their thinking and prove they've done their homework before making decisions, but you'll support them in following through

• Make clear that you'll hold them to account, with quantitative data, for the outcome of their decisions. Their responsibility isn't just doing their own job well; it's top performance from everyone who reports to them.

THIS APPROACH CAN remove the single biggest demotivator at work: the feeling that you're doing something dumb that you know isn't a good idea, but you're required to do it by your stupid boss or the company's stupid rules. If you can move to a point where professionals are given reasonable freedom to decide how to operate, but are responsible for the results, that can suddenly reveal that what you thought was a problem of work ethic was in fact a problem of motivation.

How to write your company's mission statement

IT WAS THE second time he'd asked for help. But the CEO I was coaching was having real trouble. "I'm going back and forth with my team," he said, "but we still can't get the mission right."

You can imagine the pressure he feels. Ever since Simon Sinek's influential TED talk in 2009 — arguing that great leaders inspire employees and customers by starting not with what they do or how they do it, but why — many startup founders feel they must be doing something wrong if they can't come up with a compelling mission statement and an accompanying set of values.

Big, ambitious visions can lead to big outcomes. You try to organize the world's information and make it universally accessible and useful, and you've built Google. You urge people to think different, and you've built Apple. Or you create an electric car that actually feels better than one powered by fossil fuels, and you've built Tesla. In mid-2017, investors valued Tesla about the same as General Motors, even though GM sold one hundred times as many cars.

Yet big missions and their accompanying values can easily go wrong. Facebook's declared goal — 'to give people the power to build community and bring the world closer together' —

looked less pious once it was revealed that the platform had also been used to incite genocide in Myanmar, among other sins.

And then there's Uber, which declared a 'customer obsession' as one of its values. When the company started, it declared itself opposed in principle to tipping: customers shouldn't be pressured, it argued, to give tips to cab drivers for crappy service. As it became more powerful, Uber then cranked up its 'take rate' from drivers. And when drivers began to complain that it was squeezing their earnings down towards minimum wage, the company 'solved' the problem by bringing back tipping — a neat but cynical way to use moral pressure to increase prices without taking the blame.

There are also small risks, one of which is that you might come across as hollow or insincere. The British comedian David Mitchell has a brilliant sketch satirising companies' claims of passion for everything from tax optimisation to design-conscious flooring. A better approach might be to borrow from Argentine serial entrepreneur Martin Varsavsky, who started a phone company in Spain. When he was asked at an industry conference to name his biggest customers — most people in the industry at the time thought it was important to do business with investment banks or global consultancies — he had a modest answer. "I don't have any big customers," he said. "I just have *good* customers." And he was right. The small businesses he served were less demanding, and delivered higher margins, than the JP Morgans or Accentures of the world.

So what does this mean for you, if you're running a startup?

First, decide whether the product or service you're building is one that you truly, honestly believe is destined to change the world, and is ten times better than its nearest substitute. If so, then you're in the market for an ambitious mission statement, which you'll find easy to define, since it will be obvious from the ways in which your product outclasses the alternatives.

If not, that's still OK. You can still build a top-class business in a highly competitive market that delivers terrific products, hires talented people, and provides customer service that people want to tell their friends about. Think Amazon, pre-AWS: whether or not its destiny was to be the 'Everything Store', the company was competing with other merchants in every category where it did business; it just provided a service — and over time, became much, much better.

What does this imply, then, for the mission and values you should set down and devote yourself to?

1. *Be honest and realistic.* Especially about what you have and what you can aspire to. There are too many companies out there claiming 'integrity' as their top value that are actually run by creepy slimeballs whose behaviour sets the tone for the rest of the organisation. Lucy Kellaway, the house cynic of the *Financial Times* newspaper, found that when asked, 19 out of 24 senior execs got their own companies' value statements mixed up with those of other companies.

2. *Don't overestimate what missions and values can do for the business.* Although they are in fashion, they may actually correlate negatively with performance. Kellaway showed

in a simple chart that while 83 of the top 100 companies in the FTSE index have value statements, the 17 that *don't* have one outperformed the rest by 70% over the previous ten years.

3. *Watch for the trade-offs.* When choosing values, remember that what matters more than the values themselves is the trade-offs between them. You may declare the ambition to provide amazing service to clients, have ecstatically happy staff, and deliver outstanding returns to shareholders. But what do you do when you can't have all three, and maybe not even two? One way to think about your company's values is to imagine moving a slider between apparently unrelated things. Which would you choose: being more profitable or more honest? Faster or more thorough? Kinder or more meritocratic?

4. *Ranking delivers insights.* Richard Branson, for example, doesn't put customers first; when defining his business in public, he puts employees first, and shareholders, memorably, third. If you have a set of values, their order is what's most important: it means that when employees are faced with a tough decision, they can look at the list and choose the outcome that accords closest with the top value rather than the second.

5. *Good missions can contain SMART goals.* JFK's 1961 speech arguing that the US should commit itself to "achieving the goal, before this decade is out, landing a man on the moon and returning him safely to the earth" wasn't just good rheto-

ric; it was also specific, measurable, achievable, realistic and time-bound. That's what made it SMART.

6. *Make the mission long term.* Peter Thiel's maxim that people routinely overestimate what they can achieve in a year, but routinely underestimate what they can achieve in ten years is true too for missions: think forward, and plan accordingly.

SO WHAT DO you do if you've gone through the exercise of defining your company mission and values — perhaps for the tenth time — and you still don't feel that you've nailed them?

Good execution matters every bit as much as having an inspirational mission. So rather than spend too much time agonising, simply go ahead and keep building the business. Ask yourself every day how you can serve your customers better, how you can make your product easier to use, how you can come up with ideas to make their lives more convenient that your competitors haven't thought of.

Big missions require more knowledge about the world than an early-stage startup can expect to have. The shape of the mountain range becomes visible only when you've climbed the first few foothills.

That's what happened with that CEO I was coaching. Because of the pressures of running the business, he hadn't gone out to talk to his customers for a while. His first action after our session on the company's mission was to start a new routine to pick a customer every day or two at random, and call them. This helped him discover some great insights that produced an exciting mission and an inspiring set of values.

How to resist the five
temptations of startup success

THERE ARE THREE things I feel guilty about in my business career. The one I'm ready to admit to here is this: I made an unnecessary trip on Concorde.

It was 1999, near the top of the first Internet bubble. The company I'd founded was on track for an initial public offering (IPO) within a few months, and I had a scheduling conflict: we had a board meeting in London set for one afternoon, but I was speaking at a conference in New York the next morning. It was too late for the last flight to New York, so it looked like I had to choose: move, miss or dial into the board meeting, or cancel the conference presentation. But there was a third option: go to the board, get a good night's sleep at home, and take the Concorde flight, which left Heathrow the next morning at 10am and arrived at JFK, like a magic time machine, at 8.30am the *same day*.

Since that flight cost maybe $8,000, I didn't think it would be sufficient just to get my CFO's sign-off: he reported to me, and might feel under pressure to say yes even if he had misgivings. So I emailed a board member who was one of our VC investors. He agreed, and I duly flew Concorde for the first (and last) time.

Concorde was the West's first and only supersonic commercial jet. It stopped flying in 2003, and unless the startup Boom launches a service, it has no replacement. But Concorde was cool while it lasted. There wasn't a departure gate; you simply boarded the plane straight from the Concorde lounge, which was way smarter than first class. There were lots of grand people on board, starting with a famous actress whom I didn't recognise until the third time the ground crew called her 'Lady Olivier'. In front of me was a guy in robes with a super-sized silver crucifix — likely a bigwig in the Eastern Orthodox Church— and who was accompanied by a couple of bodyguard-cardinals with smaller but still huge crucifixes and a distinct personal hygiene problem. And best of all, the sky outside the tiny windows was dark blue: we were flying at 60,000 feet, 50% higher than normal commercial jets.

But the trade-off for crossing the Atlantic in three and a half hours was that the cabin was too cramped and noisy to get much work done. And contrary to my expectation that the flight would be full of Masters of the Universe like me, travelling to their oh-so-important morning meetings in NYC, there was also a contingent who chugged a lot of Dom Perignon and were a bit too relaxed by the end of the journey. I have to admit, therefore, that it probably wasn't a great use of company money. I can't even remember what was on the agenda of the board meeting the night before, but I guess it would have been fine, and a lot cheaper, if I'd simply gone to New York the day before and dialled into the board meeting from my hotel room.

THAT'S MY CONFESSION *du jour*. But that Concorde flight was a tiny instance of the risks that startup CEOs run when their businesses flip from unknown to hot. A much, much bigger recent case in point is Adam Neumann, who built WeWork into a short-term office provider across multiple countries. But Neumann also paid himself a lot, gave jobs to family members, and had interests in some of the company's suppliers. The result was that just before the company was due to go public, having recently been renamed The We Company to reflect its ambitions to do a lot more than just provide boring old desk space, potential investors had second thoughts about the multiple layers of unusual arrangements he had in place. The company first considered cutting the valuation by more than two-thirds, but then had to pull its IPO altogether, and then to replace him as CEO.

So here's a checklist, in case your company is doing extremely well and you're starting to think you're invulnerable, of the top five things to watch out for. If you're not actually running the startup in question, but an employee or an investor, you can use it to help predict whether the CEO is in danger of having a Neumann or Kalanick-style fate.

1. *Don't spend too much money.* Yes, it's kind of obvious. But if you are running a company that's growing fast and has investors trying to throw money at you, it's easy to lose sight of reality. Your lawyers send you a $500,000 bill? No problem. The new office requires a $1m deposit? Fine. The numbers seem so big, and the decisions so swift, that smaller items like salaries, travel costs and expenses can come to seem

insignificant. And remember that investors can also go crazy. Shortly before my own company's IPO, one of our directors said something memorable at a board meeting. "The market is going to value our company at $1,000 per user," he argued. "So if we can acquire users at anything less than $1,000, we're ahead. Crank up the marketing spend!" We all nodded wisely, and I remember thinking what a great insight he'd had. Only in retrospect did I realise that it was utterly bonkers, and a symptom of the last hurrah of an overblown bull market. *Moral*: apply a reality-check to spending. If you explain it to your mother and she doesn't think it makes sense, then reconsider.

2. *Don't self-trade.* If the transactions between We and Adam Neumann (or his family members or entities he controlled) were disclosed in the S1 registration statement filed with the Securities and Exchange Commission, then we can assume they were blessed by both accountants and lawyers and therefore legal. But legal and commercially prudent aren't the same thing. If you're the founder of a hot company, then you may be able to get away with weirdo arrangements that favour you at the expense of other shareholders— for a while. But as soon as your company's angle of climb starts to level off, or heaven forbid turns into a dive, investors (and outsiders) are likely to scrutinise more closely. *Moral*: don't engage in any transactions with your startup, including salary and expenses, family members and other businesses in which you have an interest, that would embarrass you if they were splashed across the front page of the *Wall Street Journal*.

81

3.   *Seek publicity for your product, not your business.*
One of the things most intoxicating for me in the months
before our IPO was that all the media outlets that had ignored
our company for years, and had ignored our attempts to get the
message out to potential customers, suddenly became excited
about what we were doing. Ditto conferences: it soon became
clear that if I wanted, I could spend all my time flying around
the world boasting about how well the company was doing
and what a great business model it had. Only afterwards did
I realise that this isn't the kind of publicity you want. Unless
you're just about to start a funding round, and you're speaking
in a room that contains *only* people who run venture-capital
or private-equity funds with investments in your stage, space
and geography, the conference that most justifies taking a day
off work, let alone a flight, is one where you'll be speaking to
a group of customers. The opposite end of the spectrum is a
general startup event, where boasting about your unit economics will simply flag your business as a target for competitors,
and boasting about your team will prompt recruiters to try
to poach them away. *Moral*: before scheduling anything that
requires you to leave the office, ask yourself the question: how
will this outing benefit my shareholders?

4.   *Resist the temptation to build a personal brand.* The
only thing most outsiders know about your business is the
amount of money you've raised, not how fast it's growing or
how profitable it is, so one of the trappings that comes with
success (or to be precise perceived success) is an increasing
flow of inbound requests for your expertise. Would you like

to join the board of x? Sit on the government's advisory board for y? Lead the campaign for z? All these things will be fun, and they'll raise your profile. But it's worth pausing to ask how confident you are that your business will succeed. If you are so sure the job is already done that you'd happily take a year's sabbatical, then go ahead and join all those committees and sit for all those magazine photo-shoots. (Better still, maybe take the sabbatical instead of staying in your job, and spend the time reading.) If, by contrast, you still think the business has things to fix, then it's prudent to put them higher up your to-do list than making yourself more famous. *Moral*: imagine the nightmare scenario in which your company crashed and burned a year from now. Now look through your calendar for meetings or engagements in the next ninety days which you would regret having done if the business failed. Cancel them today.

5. *Don't smoke your own stuff.* In ancient Rome, victorious generals were paraded through the streets in a four-horse chariot, wearing a purple toga, laurel crown and red boots, and preceded by a procession of captives, soldiers, weapons, treasure, senators and magistrates. But accompanying the triumphant general in his chariot was an *auriga*, a special slave whose job was to stand behind, repeatedly murmuring the words *Memento mori, memento mori* — remember you are mortal. Modern translation: don't smoke your own stuff.

NOT MANY STARTUP founders — even those with a chief of staff — have anyone with the *auriga*'s responsibility. Yet it's

hugely valuable to be reminded that when you run a successful startup, you are rarely as clever, or as charming, as everyone seems to think you are. What you are, mostly, is (a) lucky,
(b) the beneficiary of great timing, and (c) hardworking.

Moral: Pay least attention to how you are viewed by people
who want to make money from your company, like bankers,
lawyers, and VCs. Pay little attention to how you are viewed
by people you've never met or who know you only a little. And
pay most attention to how you are viewed by your spouse,
your siblings, and your mother.

How to satisfy your most ambitious employees

A CEO NAMED LORRAINE began a coaching session in a panic: one of her best employees had announced that he was leaving to join a strategy consultancy — not for the pay or the stability, but for the career development.

"Should I push back?" Lorraine asked me. "I don't think career development is something people should expect in a startup."

You can see her point. Many of the benefits that come with a job at a big company — like long, structured training programs or big budgets to fly off to interesting conferences a few times a year — are expensive things that loss-making startups often can't afford. It can feel frustrating if employees expect those perks *and* to make millions from stock options if the startup works out.

So this presents Lorraine with a dilemma. Should she increase her company's costs, when she already has a limited runway? Or should she resign herself to losing good people who want career development that she can't provide?

EVERYONE WHO THINKS about their own future wants to learn new skills and to get more senior jobs in the future. But remember, mature companies have both scale and profitability. It's much cheaper for them per head to build a structured training program, because they can afford to wait longer for the returns. Investors in a startup that may not be around in two years have to think shorter term. Even if they're really confident, startups have little incentive to sink cash into training in their early months.

Different routes to professional growth

To run the numbers, think about a startup that raises its first financing from friends and family at a valuation of $2m. Spending $20,000 on training promising employees will cost 1% of the company's value. But if this cost can be put off until the business raises a seed round a year later, at a valuation of $10m, then the training cost will fall to one-fifth of a percent. And if it can be put off until a Series A two years later, when the business is worth $40m, then the cost will be only one-twentieth of a percent of the company's value. So even startup CEOs who strongly believe in training and professional development can be rational to delay spending.

Turn your lack of hierarchy into an advantage

But there's a catch in the lavish programs offered by big business. More training comes with more structure. They're often also more rigid and hierarchical: if you're a young and ambitious new employee, good luck debating a business decision with a director or VP who has been at the organization ten years. In startups, by contrast, many good founder-CEOs follow Paul Saffo's principle of 'strong opinions, weakly held.' They're willing to consider new ways of doing things, even if those new ways were discovered by an intern.

Startups have another advantage, too. In a successful venture-backed business, the size of the team can double or triple within a year or two. Then do the same again two years later. Since hiring is so hard, a known insider with proven ambition and determination can have a big advantage — and be swiftly promoted.

If an existing employee complains about the career development you offer, then have an honest chat. Help them figure out whether they'll be happy and fulfilled in this structure. If not, you should put this down to a hiring mistake, and make a mental note to be more upfront in future recruiting.

Make sure both sides understand the bargain that's being struck

But there's also stuff you can do, without loading costs on to the business, to make career development less random, more structured, and more helpful to the team. Employees can take the lead on their own career development, not the HR department. If they want the company to invest money in their future, they can show their commitment by investing their own time first. They can identify and take advantage of opportunities that are free, like reading blogs, watching TED talks, taking online courses — and proving that they're more valuable to the business as a result. This gives a company a good reason to think that investing more in them will produce great returns.

SO IF YOU'RE the CEO of a startup, what can you do to encourage and support this? Here are some approaches that I've seen succeed in different companies.

1. *Make professional development part of the evaluation process.* Ask people to report what they're doing outside work to develop their skills. Recognise and reward people investing in themselves. When employees know they're going to be asked about this, they magically start noticing opportunities that might otherwise have floated by.

2. *Don't just evaluate employees' self-managed professional development.* Support it, too. Make it part of one-on-ones. Use your experience and knowledge to give feedback on which topics people work on, and which content in those areas.

3. *Provide low-cost tools with company resources.* Even startups on a shoestring can afford books. Rather than just declare open season and let people buy whatever they want — often a recipe for a shelf full of shiny titles that never get read — invite people to ask others what they've found most useful, and buy the books that are upvoted most.

4. *Encourage people to share what they've learned. Surgeons have a phrase for it: 'see one, do one, teach one.'* When someone has just finished studying something, they're in a great position to give a 'brown-bag' 30-minute presentation on it to colleagues. This can become a regular fixture,

where the company provides the tools and drinks, and the team provides the learning.

5. *Create mentoring relationships inside the company.* There are often things that more experienced people can do in their sleep that newer hires can benefit hugely from observing. To avoid adding a big burden to employees who are already busy, be realistic about how much time you can reasonably ask them to spend on helping others. Start by halving it.

6. *Use SAAS platforms for education.* There's an amazing range of online content available for hundreds of dollars, compared with the thousands of dollars the same content used to cost when taught in offsite training seminars. Learning for twelve minutes a day isn't just less disruptive than disappearing for a week a year to take a full-time course; it can also produce better learning.

7. *Encourage team members to reach out beyond the company to learn.* It's not just CEOs that benefit from coaching. Almost everyone in the company — sales and marketing, product, engineering, finance — can learn a lot from other people in the industry. As CEO, you can prompt people to identify outsiders they can learn from, and help them figure out how to make the relationship work.

YOU MAY FEAR that none of these seven suggestions can match what might be offered by McKinsey, Procter & Gamble, or Goldman, Sachs. And you'd be right. But if you spend a couple of hours putting them together, they can combine into a career development program that isn't expensive but delivers real learning and real personal growth. That's something you can tell people about during the hiring process. It's also something that will draw in talented employees with strong self-motivation and keenness to learn.

GETTING RESULTS

How to make your
startup grow faster

A THOUSAND YEARS AGO, when a startup I'd founded was
about to IPO on the NASDAQ and the London Stock Exchange,
I built a chart of the company's monthly sales since launch,
and saw the classic curve—gently rising for a while, and then
rising a lot faster. Looking for an inflection point, I tried to
figure out what had changed the company's trajectory. But in
the month where the curve seemed to change most sharply,
what had we done differently? Nothing that I could remember.

Once the chart's y-axis was switched to a log scale, the
mystery was solved. Because then, the sales growth line
became almost magically straight. Turns out it was a simple
case of exponential growth: we'd simply grown at a constant
rate each month, and the magic of compounding had taken
effect.

I can't remember whether the sales grew at 20% or 25%
a month, but the result was that the business grew in size
by 100x or 200x over two years. After the IPO, that increase
translated directly into shareholder value: a seed investor who
had put in $100,000 later sold his shares for $21m.

Here's why this should matter to you if you're running a
startup. It may be an exaggeration to say that growth is the
only thing that matters in a startup, but only slightly. And

that's why smart VCs give disproportionate weight to growth when deciding where to put their money.

FOR A POWERFUL example, look at the brief investment memo written in September 2005 by Roelof Botha to the partners of Sequoia Capital recommending an investment in YouTube. The memo (made public in a later court case, so readable on the Internet) includes a chart showing that YouTube was growing really fast. Only a few weeks after launch, it was bigger than Vimeo and DailyMotion, its top competitors.

Botha wrote his memo on a Friday afternoon, recommending the Sequoia partners to make the company a financing offer the next Monday, and that's what they did. According to Miles Grimshaw, Sequoia invested $10m in YouTube. Thirteen months after the memo, Google bought YouTube. Sequoia's share of the proceeds: $480m.

When VCs say they like your business but "want to see more traction", that's French for "no".

If your business is growing fast, by contrast, they beat a path to your door. One CEO I coach recently raised a big Series B, and had his choice of five inbound term sheets from investors. That just may have had something to do with the fact that his company's sales grew 2.3x in the three months he was fundraising.

Most startups are different: they're growing, but not fast enough to be at a point where investors will want to put in more money by the time they run out. The result is that things look promising on the product front, but the company doesn't have the capital to keep the current team working on it. Or to put it another way, *the grass is growing but the cow is dying*.

If your reaction to this is to say that the focus on growth is unfair, some quick arithmetic may convince you why the investors are right. If your business grows 5% a month, then in two years, it will be a bit more than 3x bigger — impressive. But if it grows 20% a month, it'll be 79x bigger. And if it grows 25% a month, it'll be 212x bigger. Either of those latter two outcomes is likely to deliver what the VCs call a "fund-returner" — ie a single investment whose profits cover the investment cost of their entire fund.

This book can't tell you how to achieve those growth rates, nor what's wrong with your startup. To re-work the first line of Tolstoy's *Anna Karenina*, "All successful startups are alike. But each unsuccessful startup is unsuccessful in its own way."

But it can offer some clues as to what you need to do to change your startup's trajectory from slow to fast growth. There are seven things on the list.

1. *Build a product that people really want.* This is where it all starts, and it's harder than anything else. You know that you're not there if you're selling to businesses who say they "don't have budget", or if you have a consumer app that people download but then stop using. Product-market fit is like love; once it hits you, you'll know. To find it, you need to talk relentlessly to customers, both actual and potential. You need to look at how people use your product. You need to understand what job they're trying to do, and help them do it.

2. *Raise enough funding to pay the team you need.* It's certainly possible to build a $1bn tech company without outside funding; Basecamp, formerly known as 37 Signals, is just one of the companies who've done it. But there aren't many of them. To make your business grow, you need the right number of people with the right talents. If you have to pay for those people out of cashflow — ie out of profits from your customers — then you will have less to spend on sales and marketing, and your growth trajectory will usually be slower. A rule of thumb might be that to build and start selling a SAAS product for midsized companies, you need to pay three guys for six months. For AI-driven medical software, you may need ten people for 18 months. For an ad-supported consumer app, where you need 10m or 100m users before you start to make meaningful ad revenues, you may need to pay a team of 50 for five years. You can do the arithmetic to figure out what that means in funding — funding that has to come either from investors or from customers. Your choice.

3. *Hire people with a commitment to swift scaling.* Facebook's slogan, "Move fast and break things" (ie grow so fast that you start getting outages and problems with your service) has caused people to disagree about what things it's OK to break. Some say just about anything; others say you need to be more careful, especially with users. But what's clear is that whatever your tolerance for breakage, you need to move as fast as possible consistent with that tolerance. And your team needs to *want* to move fast. I remember a board meeting with a CEO I'd backed where we were discussing how to get

sales growing faster. The product was one that she felt needed to be shown to clients at their work, and her starting market was two districts of central London. She argued back against demos by videocall, insisting that her sales people would do better to visit in person. Each demo should take a bit less than an hour, she said. But when one investor suggested the team should target six meetings a day, since the travel time within districts might be short if the meeting were sensibly sequenced by geography, the CEO pushed back. "No," she said. "I think three meetings a day is a reasonable target." Three years later, the business is still alive, but only just. Examples of people who can't move fast are old-economy managers who need help with their email, and intellectuals who suffer from 'analysis paralysis'. Examples of people who can are common in Israel, where the IDF trains its military that if they can't get in through the door, they should abseil down the facade of the building and break in through the windows.

4. *Find a way to get strong unit economics.* One company I know has monthly costs of $50,000, an average transaction value of $200, and does 200 transactions a month. The contribution margin it makes on each transaction is $5, so its customers are contributing $1,000 a month to its fixed costs. That's miserable; the company will need to grow its sales by 50x to cover its costs today, let alone the costs of the bigger team it would need to grow. One way to get unit economics right is to raise prices. Another is to deliver your product more efficiently so your costs are lower. A third is to improve your CAC ratio — the lifetime value of a client as a multiple of the

cost of acquiring the customer (CAC). But whatever the ratio, it's also valuable to have a *quick* payback on the cost of acquiring a new customer. If your payback period is three months, then $1m raised from investors and spent on marketing can be recycled four times a year. If your payback period is a year, then you'd need to raise $4m in venture capital to grow to the same level of sales.

5.   *Built your technology in-house, not with an outsource dev shop.* First-time entrepreneurs are often tempted to get an agency to build their minimum viable product. This usually doesn't work out. Products are rarely right first time around, especially if they're built using a waterfall rather than agile approach. To get to product-market fit, you should expect to make lots of frequent, incremental changes. An agency who built you a minimum viable product at a fixed price will usually make its margins on the 'amends', so the price will go up sharply. And they're not likely to be available either at the speed you need. That's why it's worth giving a chunk of equity to the CTO who will build the first version of the product, and will have a good reason to take your call at 10pm on a Friday night if something urgently needs fixing.

6.   *Use your OKRs.* When you're bogged down in the nitty-gritty of day-to-day problems with your business, it's easy to forget what's important. In those moments, you can turn to the OKRs you wrote at the start of the month or quarter, using them like the stars in navigation: they tell you which direction to head in.

7. *Commit to experimenting.* When startup founders talk about their 'runway', they usually mean the number of months they have left before running out of cash. But the best way to measure your runway isn't by time, it's by number of experiments. Most startups don't hit product-market fit, and are still trying to find it when they have to close down. Yet the experiments themselves aren't the most expensive thing. Salaries and rent account for more than half of most startup costs. So if you can find a way to get twice as many experiments done in the same time, that's like doubling the length of your runway. Brainstorm a list of potential improvements to all parts of your business. Set up a method to rigorously test them, treating the potential improvement as the challenger and the status quo as the control. Run the tests as quickly as you can consistent with getting good data, and make immediate changes based on what you learn. A successful challenger becomes the new control.

IF YOU'RE A seasoned startup founder, many of the things on this list may seem obvious. But if your startup isn't growing as fast as you would like, you may find it valuable to look back and force yourself to admit how many of the things on the list you're actually doing.

And if you doubt the potential of these things to be transformative, here's a back-of-the-envelope example. To increase your business 100x in two years requires 21.2% growth each month. If each month you increase by 5%
- The number of people who see your product
- The percentage of those people who give you contact

details

- The percentage of those who buy
- The frequency with which they subsequently purchase
- And their average basket size

then you can *more than* hit that 21.2% number.

SMALL CHANGES ACROSS many parts of your business, executed diligently over time, can turn a low-growth startup into a high-growth startup.

How well-chosen objectives
can empower your employees

IN ONE OF my favourite cartoons, Dilbert's pet dog asks him, "How was work?"

"Are you being sarcastic?" Dilbert demands. "You know my life is an endless series of useless tasks orchestrated by idiots. Why do you even ask?"

"I like hearing it," says the dog.

"Your honesty is not refreshing," replies Dilbert.

NOT MANY OF the CEOs I coach have this problem. Running a venture-backed startup is a job that gives you a strong sense of purpose, a feeling that you're learning new stuff every day, and great autonomy in how you do things. From the founder's desk, the company's strategy often seems clear as glass, and the connection between the mission and everyone's jobs is unmistakable. Some tasks may be boring or repetitive, but they're usually either part of the business model (eg driving for Uber), or a temporary measure that's part of a 'concierge MVP' — manual processes that the company expects to automate, because you learn a lot from having people do something by hand before you write code to do it. So when you're at the top of the pyramid, it takes some effort to understand how things feel further down.

That's where Scott Adams's strip comes in. For even in a startup with 25 to 100 people, that crystalline vision can get muddied by the time it's filtered down to the intern's daily responsibilities.

THINGS CAN FAIL in two ways. One is that a job might be important and closely connected to the company's mission, but the person doing it doesn't understand why. The other is that your workers are right: the tasks they're doing are indeed pointless — they know enough about the processes or the customers to know that there's a better way to solve the business problem. But this insight hasn't bubbled upwards to the CEO, so the company is missing an opportunity to improve a wasteful and poorly-designed process.

Whether your team members are right or wrong in thinking their work is pointless, you still have a problem to fix. That, in a nutshell, explains the value of OKRs — the system of 'objectives and key results' that Andy Grove implemented at Intel during the 1960s and 1970s, and that made its way to Google, where Larry Page credited it with helping the company to grow 10x many times over.

John Doerr, the VC at Kleiner Perkins who learned OKRs at Intel and then taught them to Google, wrote a good book about them called *Measure What Matters*. But you can sum up OKRs in a sentence: setting an objective that is a clearly-defined goal, and one or more key results that are clearly-defined measures to track whether that objective has been achieved.

THE POWER OF the process comes from the combination of the O and the KR. You need to set an objective so that everyone in the team has a clear idea of what you're trying to achieve. And you need key results to hold yourselves rigorously accountable for the progress you're making towards that goal. As Doerr puts it, "Did I do that or did I not do it? Yes? No? Simple. No judgments in it." Which means you need to draft your KRs with some care. So 'Run a pilot with x people to test y', which sounds precise, actually isn't specific enough. Does 'run a pilot' mean start the pilot by the end of the quarter? Or ended? Or end it? Or analyse the results?

In a well-run business, both the objectives and the key results have worked their way all the way from top to bottom. Everyone knows what they're supposed to be doing and why they're doing it.

People lazily use the metaphor of 'rowing in the same direction' in business. It's not just about direction. It's also about the timing. There's little point running an amazing marketing campaign if the product isn't ready.

When I was in college, I competed as part of an eight-man rowing team. When everyone pulls in perfect rhythm, the result is truly astonishing: the boat speeds through the water faster than you'd imagine possible, with a firm push in your back at each stroke. The same is true for startup teams: if you get both direction and timing right, the difference is striking.

There's plenty of advice out there on how to implement OKRs inside companies (and I've written a separate chapter on how to complete them -- see page 107). But stepping back from the operational detail, I'd suggest five things are particularly important in making sure that they're implemented successfully.

1. *Have you held an all-hands offsite to explain and discuss your company's objectives?* If you're the CEO, then setting your company's strategy is one of your three most important jobs. You'll spend a lot of time thinking about it; if anyone can articulate clearly what your company is trying to achieve, then that person should be you. But what about everyone else? Most other employees in the company will have little input into strategy, so even dedicated people will be tempted to tune out when it's discussed, since they've got plenty to think about in their own day-to-day responsibilities.

That's why it's so important to get everyone together periodically and explain to them your current take on how your company can be successful and what you think you need to do to get there. Then, once you've got everyone's attention, you can ask them what *they* think. If you frame the discussion in the right way, even people with little experience or technical or financial knowledge can contribute interesting and useful ideas that can improve your approach. But you can't do this while everyone's trying to do their normal day job. Hence one of the CEOs I work with holds a 'Straturday' every half year, in which team members get paid to come in on a weekend day to discuss strategy and objectives offsite. Another has a quarterly half-day meeting in the office, where everyone stops what they're doing to take part.

2. *Do you often remind your team of what your objectives are?* Since strategy is part of your job description, nobody needs to remind you what objectives you set for the current quarter. If you're a typical startup CEO, they'll be imprinted in your subconscious. But even if your company has regular offsites where you outline and discuss your objectives, it's not realistic to expect everyone to remember them between sessions especially if your company is growing. So you need to take lots of opportunities to remind people. If you get the team together and *nobody* in the room groans when you remind everyone of the company's objectives, then you're probably not telling them often enough. A bit like restaurants: if your restaurant always has a queue outside but nobody complains about the prices, then they're too low.

3. *Do you help your reports translate company-level objectives into objectives for their own departments?* Strategy consultants at McKinsey are fond of the 'MECE' principle, of taking a big task and breaking it down into lots of smaller tasks. MECE means 'mutually exclusive' (ie, the tasks are separate from each other) and 'collectively exhaustive' (ie, when you've done all the small tasks, you've achieved the big task). That's a good way to think about company objectives: a startup has a 'big, hairy goal', but that goal needs to be translated into separate quarterly or monthly objectives for marketing, sales, product, tech, operations, finance and so on.

Many CEOs assume the heads of those departments will be able to intuit from the high-level objective what their team needs to do to contribute. But that's a heroic assumption. It's possible to be pretty good at any one of those functional leadership jobs without fully seeing the big picture and figuring out how to draft the department's objectives so they tightly match the company's overarching objectives.

This means it's the CEO's role to help. Rather than just leave department heads to come up with their own objectives, it makes sense to work with them to ensure their ideas align with your top-level vision for the company. Call it coaching or brainstorming, or call it what you will, but you need to be in there supporting your reports so the objectives they set are right. An hour spent helping the head of marketing craft exactly the right set of plans repays itself a hundredfold when the plans are executed.

4. *Do you help your managers train their own teams in setting objectives and key results?* It's one thing for the head of marketing to have a clear idea what the department needs to achieve over the coming quarter. It's another thing for every person in the marketing team to know what they need to do. Again, setting objectives is a valuable skill for people to learn, but they can't be expected to learn it unaided. So just as it's the CEO's job to make sure the head of marketing has the right objectives for their department, so also it's the head of marketing's job to make sure all the people in the marketing team have the right personal objectives. If you want it to be done well, you need to be asking the people who report to you about how they're cascading objectives downwards, and getting them to discuss individual cases with you openly. That's the only way you'll be able to tell whether individual

contributors are being given the right guidance, and the only way to see how effectively managers are leading their teams.

5. *Are you prepared for problems and mistakes in cascading objectives through the company?* Using the framework of OKRs isn't immediately intuitive or easy. It requires high levels of abstract thought about where you want your company to be in the future, combined with the practical consideration of the small-scale tasks that individuals do and how those tasks will contribute to the outcome. That's exactly like the way in which the strength, technique and timing of individual rowers contributes to the speed and smoothness of a 19-metre boat.

ONCE YOU EFFECTIVELY integrate the communication of objectives into your team, you may still meet people who describe their jobs as 'an endless series of useless tasks orchestrated by idiots'. But at least those people won't work for *your* company.

How to actually complete
your OKRs once they're set

THANKS TO GOOGLE — and ultimately to the late, great
Andy Grove — lots of startup founders use the OKRs to focus
on what's most important and to get stuff done.

But there's a problem. Many founders find that using OKRs
for setting objectives is one thing, but actually achieving them
is another. "My upcoming week is pretty full," said Helena,
one of the Series A CEOs I coach. "Today I've got four one-on-
ones, two team meetings, and a board call to prepare for. I
don't know where my time goes, but somehow I feel I'm not
actually spending it on what's important."

The same thing happened to me in my work as a VC: I was
repeatedly getting only a low percentage of my OKRs done.

The underlying causes became visible only after looking
back on the past month or quarter, and analysing how my
working time was spent. I'd allowed inbound demands on my
time to take precedence, and had often chosen easy wins like
clearing my email over what was most important.

As Stephen Covey points out in his book *First Things
First*, it's important to remember that if you're trying to fill a
big glass jar, it makes sense to put in the rocks first, then the
gravel, and then the sand. Smaller items find their own space
around the big ones. If you do it the other way round — if you

start your day with email, then you may never get to the big things. If the sand goes in first — in the form of email, phone calls, meetings, random questions from your reports — there will be no room for the rocks.

When you use an OKR system, those rocks are the tasks that will achieve your key results. These tasks cascade down to departments and then to individual employees — because by definition, those are the things you've decided must be achieved even if everything else drops off the bottom of the list.

Over time, I've evolved a way of connecting those tasks to my daily schedule that has helped me sharply raise the percentage of my key results that get achieved. I haven't seen anyone else do this, but here is how it works.

1. *First, translate your key results into tasks.* Some KRs are done by definition when a single task is complete. Others translate into a handful of tasks. So if the key result is hiring a VP sales, then the tasks required to achieve it might be: design the hiring process; set up software to manage it; write the job spec and share on social media; do 15-minute screening calls with 16 candidates; do one-hour in-person interviews with five candidates; and do three 20-minute calls with the successful candidate to negotiate their terms. Once you have a list of tasks, write down how many hours each task will take. Most people, like me, are 'time optimists'; bear this in mind when estimating, but don't worry too much because you'll be able to correct this later.

2. *Next, work out how much time you have available.*
You might think you have eight, ten, or twelve hours a day
to work on your key results in the coming month or quarter.
But you don't. Many inbound demands on your time are
important things that can't be neglected. So you need to make
a reasonable estimate of how many hours a day you have
available, after dealing with all those things. Figure out how
many working days you have in the coming month or quarter
(exclude conferences, off-sites, public holidays, work travel,
vacations and other days out of the office). Then multiply that
number by the available hours per day. That tells you how
many hours in total you really have to work on your OKRs.

3. *Now take a reality check.* Is the number of hours
required for the tasks on your list more than the number of
hours you actually have available? If it is, then your chance of
hitting your key results is approximately zero, unless you find
a way to go without sleep or suddenly become twice as productive as you've ever been in your life. So go back to the OKRs,
and prune the list back to what's achievable. Don't worry, if
you turn out to be Superman after all, you can add some more
tasks later.

4. *Put the tasks in your calendar.* Once you have a realistic list of tasks, pruned back to the time you actually have
available, you have what looks like a daunting to-do list. But
one small thing can make that list seem suddenly manageable:
you can actually put the tasks into your calendar as if they
were appointments. So you might schedule like this:

*   Two hours starting 11am on Monday for setting up the

hiring process
- Two hours for the job spec from 2pm on Tuesday
- Four hours for the screening calls, split over two slots on Wednesday and Thursday of the following week
- Interviews at 9am every day of the week after that
- Calls with the successful candidate at 5:30pm on Monday, Wednesday and Friday of the final week of the month.

The key point is that the tasks are now in your diary. Now, instead of having a terrifyingly big and complex project to achieve, you've simply got to do each day whatever is in your calendar. And if someone asks you for help on something, or an interesting opportunity comes up, you'll have to face the fact that accepting the request will stop you from doing the task you had scheduled, and so your key result won't get achieved unless you find some other place in your calendar to put it.

5. *Resist the temptation to postpone.* Some of the tasks will be easy to stick to (like a scheduled call, where there's moral pressure from the other person to show up). Others (like writing without interruption) will be tempting to postpone, and in the past you've often allowed more urgent but less important things to be scheduled on top.

When faced with these temptations, I try to remind myself that working effectively is all about learning how to let decisions be made by the 'future you', who wants what's best for you in the long term, over the 'present you'. For some people, the present you wants to lie in bed, eat cookies and waste time on social media. But the present you is still a danger if you're conscientious. It's the you that wants a tidy desk, an empty inbox, and lots of other things done whose business value is above zero, but definitely not the highest.

You've put the tasks for your OKRs into your calendar for a reason: you've decided that if you do nothing else this month or this quarter, you definitely want to do those things. What happens when a meeting request comes in? Many startup founders assume that if a client or investor proposes a meeting time, they've got to treat it as a take-it-or-leave-it. In fact, if you ask nicely to do it at another time, they're often able to.

So you need to distinguish between competing claims on your time. Some have a mixture of urgency and importance that truly takes priority (such as dropping everything to convince a valued team member who's received an outside job offer to stay). Others don't. Ask yourself how this competing claim rates against your original plan, and write down the answer.

6. *Keep a record of when you miss your OKR tasks.* In cases where you can't give priority to the future you, then edit the missed appointment for the task to start with 'ND', meaning not done, so you can easily see at the end of each week which tasks you missed, and then reschedule them. I use Zapier to put all those appointments tagged with ND into a spreadsheet so I can track progress in the never-ending battle between my present and future selves.

7. *Check in on your OKRs at the end of each week.*

Update your list to show which tasks have been achieved and how close you came to sticking to your schedule. When you do, you may get an unpleasant surprise, and suddenly realise that the tasks you scheduled and the OKRs they represented don't seem right any more. That's all right. Maybe your first cut wasn't sufficiently considered, or the combination of new information and time to reflect has changed your mind. View the process as a reality check, and if you make a change to the OKRs or the tasks, write down what change you made and why you did it. As you do this more regularly and reliably, you'll get better at it.

The weekly check and review of the tasks that you promised yourself you would do but actually marked as not done also forces you in real time to face your own inability to stick to your commitments. This is uncomfortable, but no bad thing. And sometimes, with increasing frequency if you stick to this process, it gives you a little reward — a tiny dopamine hit for completing a few tasks, and hitting an objective. This focuses and energises you to stick to your commitments.

8. *Review your OKRs at the end of each cycle.* At the end of each OKR cycle, whether it's monthly or quarterly, go back and review how you did, focusing on what percent done each key result is and what the total achievement rate is across everything.

How to learn from reviewing last month's OKRs

Mike is one of the most talented CEOs that I coach. A former strategy consultant who speaks three languages, he's built a thriving service marketplace business in a highly competitive sector, and he's successfully raised three funding rounds from top investors, the most recent of which delivered a lump of new money a few months ago.

With that in place, Mike decided to get more serious about how he runs the business. He held a session with the people who reported to him, agreed on a set of objectives and key results, and got going. After one quarter, he felt energised: there was much greater clarity in the team about what the company was trying to do, and he felt the pace had accelerated. But Mike had some doubts. Were the objectives the right ones? Did the key results match? Could he run the process any better for the next quarter?

That's why we set up a session to review progress once the quarter was complete. The material we had in front of us was the objectives that the company set for the period, the key results designed to measure whether those objectives had been achieved, and then separate sets of OKRs showing each department contribution to what the company was trying to achieve during the period. Out of our review came seven questions which can usefully be applied in other contexts where OKRs are used.

1. *Did these OKRs take us towards our destination?* It's tempting to see this as banal: Of course they did, you answer; that's why we chose them. But in some ways, OKRs are like to-do lists on steroids. And if you've tried different ways of keeping to-do lists, you'll have had the weird experience of coming across an old to-do list from some time ago, and peering, puzzled, at the items on it, many of which have been superseded or no longer seem relevant today. *What the heck was this?*, you ask yourself. Why on earth did I think that mattered? If you discuss your old OKRs with your co-founders, management team or coach, you may conclude that the old objectives are no longer the right ones. Don't spend any time beating yourself up about why you got them wrong. Often, it's simply new information that makes clear what your destination should be.

2. *Have the OKRs been effectively cascaded down to departments and people?* Phrases like 'getting everyone on the same page' or 'pulling in the same direction' have become so familiar that they're clichés. Elon Musk famously says that people in your company are vectors, and that your progress is the sum of all vectors. Vectors have magnitude and direction — and if they're directionally different, that's a waste of effort. Your mission as CEO is to ensure that you align all the vectors to point the same way. That means checking carefully through the list of department and individual OKRs to make sure that each one of them corresponds precisely (not vaguely) to a higher-level company OKR. If it doesn't, it's wasted effort.

3. *Are your key results, in combination, sufficient?* A set

of OKRs might be necessary but still not sufficient to get you to your desired destination. For instance, at Mike's company one KR for the quarter was to increase contribution dollars by 15%. That may sound impressive: compounding at that pace over a year would result in a contribution increase of just under 75%. But 75% wouldn't actually get Mike's company where it would need to be in order to raise the next round 18 months from now. To achieve that, Mike would need a 21% per month increase in contribution. There were good business reasons for setting a lowish bar in the first set of OKRs. But if Mike wanted to achieve what he needed for his business, the plan needed revamping.

4.   *Does each key result accurately reflect its matching objective?* Mike's company had some technical issues with an unreliable app. One objective was (challengingly) defined as *Restore faith in the product*, and its top key result was to increase test coverage (the proportion of the total lines of code in its software for which 'unit tests' had been written) to a specified percentage. That KR was duly achieved. But the wisdom of a quarter's hindsight revealed that fixing bugs alone wasn't really what the problem was about. The objective should really have been phrased as *Ensure that our product offers a compelling proposition to our customers*. And that objective wasn't yet achieved, for business rather than technical reasons. Rephrasing it for the next quarter wasn't just semantics. It helped to clarify what the company's founders and management needed to get right.

5.   *Are we addressing the symptom or the problem?* In

Mike's marketplace business, one challenge has been that the sellers don't respond reliably enough to the buyers — they get messages about possible transactions, but often ignore them. So last quarter, the company set as one KR to implement an experiment 'forcing' buyers to give a response, just as Uber demands that you rate your last driver before you can book another. If Mike's plan succeeded, it could force the sellers to decline transactions explicitly, but it wouldn't give any insight into why they had done so. Was it because the transaction wasn't economically advantageous to them? Because they had a concern about the buyer? Or some misgiving about the service? That's why it's a good idea, when updating OKRs from quarter to quarter, to ask the tough questions: What's the real problem here? And is what we're doing really directed at solving that problem?

6. *Is this objective the best one to do now, or could we get a better result by doing something else first?* Graphic design was one of Mike's polymathic talents, so his company had never used a professional branding agency. Both its name and its logo were his own work, and they were pretty good. But they could be better, his team felt, and so one set of OKRs was set around the idea of refreshing them: an objective of redefining the brand, and a key result of shortlisting three agencies to pitch on the work.

Sounds great, right? Well, yes. But Mike knew that the biggest challenge he faced in getting the company towards the long-term goal of making it huge and profitable was to fix its unit economics — to make more money on each transaction, so that advertising and marketing could be more swiftly recycled and capital used more efficiently. The rebrand could help with this, but it could also wait a few quarters. Other projects might have a higher payoff if done sooner.

7. *Which objectives have the biggest quantitative effect on the outcome?* Which leads to the final question. Many things in companies can't be captured in numbers. But some things can. And when you're faced with a long list of possible things you could do, and the knowledge that you don't remotely have the resources to do them all, pick the metric that matters most for you — in Mike's case, unit economics. And when you're kicking around ideas for what to include in the next quarter's OKRs, ask what effect each idea might have on that key metric, if achieved with the outcome you hope. If you can find another objective with an equal probability of success that would have a bigger effect, then you know which one to put on your list.

THE USE OF objectives and key results is a valuable management tool in startups. But like many other tools, it's not fire-and-forget. To get the best from OKRs, you need to think fresh thoughts every time about where you're trying to go and how you plan to get there. These questions helped Mike figure out what his new set of OKRs should be. With luck, they should help you too.

MANAGING PEOPLE

How to manage people
who report to you

'I'M EXHAUSTED,' SAID Leo. 'I didn't have much of a weekend.'

Since Leo is one of the CEOs I coach, I already knew he was fundraising. 'Were you working on the pitch deck?' I asked.

'Nope, that was Sunday,' he replied. 'I spent Saturday in the office, working with the phone-sales team.'

At the time, Leo's company had raised over $20m and it had over 50 employees. It had a VP Sales, and underneath her a manager for the phone-sales team. So what the heck was the CEO doing in the office on Saturday, working with a group of people who report to someone two levels below him?

'I'd done some data analysis,' said Leo. 'I noticed that our sales on Saturdays were much lower than other days of the week. There was obviously a problem that needed fixing, and Julia, my VP Sales, was away for a few days. But don't worry — I called her beforehand to check she was OK with me dealing with it.'

'How did it work out?'

'I learned a lot. Two of the sales people showed up a couple of hours late. And they clearly weren't motivated. With me there and supporting them, the sales numbers for the day were way higher than usual — and I'm confident that the increase will continue for the rest of this month.'

'How did Julia take it when she came back?'

'Well, obviously I had to explain the situation, since the sales team reported to the sales manager, and the sales manager reported to her as VP sales. But she was fine. No complaints.'

'Leo, I remember in your last job, there was a time when the CEO stepped in to fix a problem in your department. How did you feel about that?'

'Yeah, it was terrible. So demoralising. But this was different.'

'How?'

There was a long pause.

'I see,' said Leo quietly.

LET'S NOT GIVE Leo too hard a time. His heart was in the right place. He wanted the best for the company. He had the imagination to research the data to identify the problem. He had the determination to fix it right away. And he had the commitment to show up himself over the weekend and work with the people at the coal face. Not many CEOs could claim the same.

And yet, his intervention wasn't helpful for the long term. In his previous job, Leo hated the boss who kept interfering in areas of his responsibility. This time around, he was gentler and more polite when he did the same to Julia, his VP sales. But the effect was the same: both she and the sales manager beneath her felt *less* motivated. Why bother to troubleshoot problems in my department, they probably thought to themselves, if Leo's going to swoop in over the weekend and fix them for me?

But the greatest harm from Leo's actions was done to Leo himself. He was making his own job harder: adding stuff to his to-do list, increasing the number of things he needed to be aware of, reducing the time he had available for stuff that *only* the CEO could do.

As we discussed the issue, Leo made it clear that he was aware of all these problems. Yet he simply couldn't see an alternative to stepping in if he needed to get those Saturday sales up. What he needed was a structure to help him get the problem solved — but without solving it himself.

Over the next few weeks, I asked a number of other CEOs I work with what they thought were the most successful tools for managing their teams. The response was unanimous: one-on-one meetings. I tried to identify the common features of what they do and say in these meetings, and summarised them into one simple, easy-to-remember framework: SCRIM.

Scrims are often used in theatres: they look like a solid curtain when lit from in front while you're waiting for the play to begin, but then they become transparent when the stage lights go up — and you realise that you can actually see what's going on behind the barrier.

In some ways, that's a perfect metaphor for what goes on in a one-on-one (OOO) meeting with someone who reports to you: sitting in a room with just them, you can't directly see what they're doing to manage the people who report to them, but if you ask the right questions, you can get a pretty clear idea of what it's like behind the scrim when they're managing their team.

I wish I could claim credit for the poetic choice of word, but in fact it's simply an acronym to help you remember a list of five topics. When you have someone reporting to you, your mission is to verify, step by step, that everything they need to succeed is in place: the right Selection, the right Coaching, the right Reliability, the right Involvement, and the right Monitoring. In short, SCRIM.

1. *Selection.* When you hire new people, you expect to need to teach them some of the skills needed to do the job. But if they don't have the basic capacities — being good with people in a sales job, or being numerically literate in an analytical job — then the training needed to allow them to perform well is going to take ages and cost a lot (if indeed it can succeed at all).Unfortunately, startup CEOs aren't immune to making mistakes in selection. Yet most nice people don't like firing, and consequently are unable to deal with those mistakes. It's *your* job as CEO to get your managers to talk about their teams, and discuss whether they have what the company needs now. If not, then you need to fix your recruitment process. But meanwhile, you'll need a humane way to replace them with someone better suited. Usually, the manager they report to will need to do the firing. Often, you'll need to help; with a less experienced manager, you may need to be in the room when the meeting happens.

2. *Coaching.* Once the manager has the right people, they need to make sure they're properly trained. And to do that, the manager needs to have a clear list of the skills required plus

a defined process for making sure the people have learned them. If the manager can't show you the list and the process, then that probably means there's a serious training project to do. If they can show you, then you can help troubleshoot it by asking questions about the fit between what the business needs and what the people are being taught.

3. *Reliability.* In most organisations, there's a set of processes and routines that people need to go through in order to do the job properly — whether it's an office manager going through a checklist when they open the doors in the morning, or a senior sales person following up after a meeting with an important client. If those processes are clearly defined, then there's much more chance that things will be done properly. As discussed on page 246, checklists are vital in achieving consistent, watertight processes. You know you've achieved Reliability when someone who is the right Selection and has the right Coaching delivers to a high standard day in, day out.

4. *Involvement.* If people in the organisation are going to perform well, they don't just need to know what to do; they also have to want to do it. And that means the company needs to give them the right incentives. Money is the most obvious one: getting the commission structure right is crucial in any sales function. But there are lots of other issues at stake. Are people getting enough recognition? Enough autonomy? Are they being rewarded for high performance rather than for politicking? Get the incentives right, and people will start identifying problems for themselves and solving them. They'll feel involved in the company's success or failure.

5. *Monitoring.* Even with the right selection, training, routines and incentives, it's still important that department managers are checking from day to day and week to week how things are going. That's more subtle than it looks. The old line attributed to management guru Peter Drucker is that 'what gets measured gets managed'. But that can have perverse results: if managers monitor the wrong measures, as Jerry Muller explains in his book *The Tyranny of Metrics*, then they tilt people's behaviour to optimising for them. So one of your tasks as CEO is to make sure your managers are measuring the right things.

WHICH BRINGS THE discussion full circle. SCRIM isn't just something you want to make sure your reports do to their teams. You also need to use it on yourself in assessing how you run your team. One way to hold yourself to account is with a coach, or (if you're lucky enough to have an investor who's sufficiently engaged and experienced and has the time available) with a board member. But if you can't get either of those things, then simply scheduling an hour a week and an extra hour every month to sit quietly in a room, go through the SCRIM checklist, write notes, and think about the people that report to you one by one. This can help you become a much better CEO.

How to ask your reports
good questions

"SHE WAS THE best boss I ever worked for," said James. "She didn't interfere at all in what I was doing. But she asked me questions every time we met — and those questions made me hugely better at my job."

We were in the middle of a coaching session. James is the CEO of a fast-growing tech startup, prodigiously talented and indefatigably hardworking. But he hasn't had much experience managing other people. He's still learning how to be a good boss.

One of the most vivid things that came out of our discussion was getting James to talk about his own experiences when he'd been managed by other people. There was the manager who disappeared for what felt like weeks on end, leaving him to make decisions without support but then returning, looking disappointed when things didn't turn out exactly as expected. And there was the one who checked up on everything, five times a day, telling James not only what to do but how, in excruciating detail.

But the manager who taught James, the most, paradoxically, was the one who asked him the best questions. Questions are great if they're asked the right way. They help you resist the temptation to judge the situation before you understand it. They prompt the other person to find an answer for themselves, rather than do what they're told. And they help you listen more.

THE NEED FOR good questions is especially urgent in start-ups. When they're successful, they grow like weeds, and it's hard to stay organised when half the staff has been in the job for less than six months. When you have a group of people reporting to you who are each in turn responsible for a team of other people, your biggest job is to make sure that they're managing their teams competently. And that typically requires you to cover a lot of ground in a short time.

As explained on page 120, SCRIM is a framework of five topics that managers can check with the people who report to them: Selection, Coaching, Reliability, Involvement and Monitoring. But how do you turn the five into an agenda, and how do you avoid telling your reports what to do? Here are some questions that can help you do that.

1. *Who's your best performer this week, and who's having the most trouble?* Most people are kind, and so instinctively recoil from firing people. This means that hiring mistakes — bringing in unsuitable people — often take much longer to recognise and fix than they should.

Given that resources devoted to coaching and training are wasted on the wrong people, Selection is arguably the most important agenda topic — but unless you want to acquire the reputation of a crazed axeman, don't ask people straight out who in their team is incompetent and needs to be fired.

With the questions phrased as above, you can help your managers get in the habit of speaking honestly to you about how their people are doing. And if you simply wait rather than diving in with your own view — perhaps asking the occasional 'What else?' if the person you're meeting dries up — then they will often give you surprising detail which you can file away for later.

Once you've verified that the manager has made a serious attempt at training any team member who is in doubt, you're ready for a discussion at a future meeting of whether the under-performing team member is right for the job.

2. *What skills do they need that they don't have, and how could you help them become more independent?* These questions address the Coaching issue; they force the person reporting to you to think about whether they've trained their team adequately and what that training should consist of. When a manager feels overworked or claims that their team is incompetent, lack of attention to training is often the under-lying issue.

Recently, one CEO said to me that the ideal report would be someone who could just be left to get on with it. I don't agree. If they can need absolute zero support, they probably have the skills to be much more senior, and you'll therefore be paying for a far more experienced person than you need.

If you want talented people at low cost, try to make your company the place where they *learned the most* and *grew fastest*.

3. *What do you expect your team to do every day and every week, and how consistent do you feel their execution is?* These questions address the reliability issue. If a thoracic surgeon with ten years' training still needs a checklist to avoid mistakenly leave a scalpel or a sponge inside the patient's chest, then it's unrealistic to expect that someone two years out of college is going to perform with 100% reliability every time.

It's their manager's job to help define a set of habits (maybe at the start and end of each day and week), so they'll learn over time to zip through tasks quickly and ensure that nothing falls through the cracks. Habit-stacking (see page 252) can help here.

Defining a checklist is an issue of process design that requires a particular 'system mindset', and most individual contributors (and many managers) can't do it for themselves. It's your job to make sure managers design the right processes for their people. And to help them if necessary.

4. *Who in your team is most likely to quit, who's most enthusiastic, how's morale, and what could you do to improve it?* These questions address the issue of Involvement, or how engaged people really are in their jobs. The first few times you ask, they'll often uncover process problems. One CEO I work with discovered that sales people were taking precious time after each call to write up notes in their CRM, simply because they didn't have headsets that allowed them to type during calls. And after that, the questions may also uncover compen-

sation issues: X wants a pay rise, Y wants a promotion, Z wants a bonus or more stock options.

But financial compensation is often a substitute for broader satisfaction at work — that's why investment banks pay so well. Your questions can help reveal and then fix internal politics, personal animosities, and wider or more existential concerns.

Over time, you can broaden out from discussing just the most and least motivated. Good managers will have a sense of the morale of every individual working for them, and they ought to be able to report to you on it.

5.   *What numbers tell you how well things are going in your department? What needs to be fixed? How do you predict what your results will be next week or next month?* These are great questions for Monitoring, and they'll have a bewildering range of answers from contacts per day or close rate in sales to Fibonacci points per sprint in software development.

The important thing is this: once you know the measures that reveal how well things are going, you're in a position to home in on the biggest problems first and fix them, rather than making your team prepare exhaustive updates.

Only rarely can you expect managers to identify the right metrics themselves. That's often your job. But monitoring doesn't work best imposed from above. When your reports feel that they had a hand in deciding what indicators to watch, you're likely to get more engagement from them in meeting their targets.

A good rule of thumb is to ask people for their ideas on what to measure and how. If they come up with an idea that's obviously not going to work, no need to tell them; simply wait. Ask them for another idea — and then, when they've come up with three choices, invite them to assess the pros and cons of each. Well-chosen metrics or KPIs are immediately actionable: the number tells you what problem you need to solve.

YOU'LL PROBABLY BE able to come up with lots more questions that will fit your company and your context better. But the key thing is that they should be questions, not instructions or suggestions. The more you put the problem in front of someone who reports to you and ask them to solve it, the more you're helping them get better at their job rather than doing their job for them. And the more you'll be like James's memorably inspiring, best-ever boss.

How to get your team
to talk to you

THE EMAIL CAME in from Jonas, one of the smartest CEOs I know. "I'm having real trouble with some of my one-on-ones," he said. "It happens with people who are shy and not particularly open. But I have to keep asking them questions, and they mostly give brief answers. How can I get them to have a proper discussion?"

Jonas isn't alone. A number of the startup CEOs I work with have found it hard to get their team to talk to them. A few people will ask for guidance and input on every single tiny thing. Others get defensive fast — or like Jonas's people, they close off discussion by giving out the least possible information. And some, when asked direct questions, will respond with generalities like "Don't worry, it's all under control."

What's going wrong here?

A GOOD STARTING-POINT, IF you're a CEO or a senior manager, is to put yourself in the shoes of people who report to you. Remember how intimidating it can be to be interrogated about what you've been doing — especially if the questions start with the word *why*, which a listener can mishear as carrying a subtext of *you idiot*. If it goes the wrong way, the interrogation can reveal that you've made mistakes, that you don't know what to do going forward, and you're not doing a good job of managing your team.

Senior people are used to accounting for what they are working on, and answering questions about it. So if you've been held to account yourself, you'll have absorbed by osmosis the skill of asking good questions. But younger founders have often had only minimal experience of working for someone else — so they find it particularly hard to be aware of what it's like on the other side of the table. Remember, also, that CEOs are more confident than the average member of the population. Since they don't find it intimidating to be questioned, they often find it hard for them to see why lesser mortals might.

The middle three elements of SCRIM — Coaching, Reliability, Involvement — are all collaborative and constructive, where people have every reason to be open with their managers. But the first and last — checking Suitability and Monitoring — are a hornet's nest. You can't realistically expect someone to hand over information if they think it might risk getting them fired. That's why it can be valuable to take those two elements out and deal with performance appraisals and metrics in separate meetings.

Once you've done that, there are a few things you can do to make the meeting as comfortable as possible for the person reporting to you.

• Schedule your OOOs, and stick to the schedule. Some CEOs cancel them frequently, because they allow any old external meeting to take precedence. Others don't schedule them at all: they just spontaneously grab the person they want to meet and take them into a conference room. If you take those approaches, you're signalling to your report that the meeting isn't important to you. If that's the case, no wonder if they come unprepared.

• Ensure you meet in a quiet place, with no interruptions. To help stay fully engaged, you can 'forget' to bring your phone.

• Avoid setups that feel hierarchical or confrontational. Behind your desk while they sit in a chair in front of you: bad. Side by side on a sofa: good. Available drinks or snacks can't hurt.

• Send positive body-language signals by adopting their posture. Don't forget to smile.

Although it's tempting to ease into the discussion with small talk about weekends, sports or social life, there's actually a better way: ask a simple question to find out what's on their mind, and listen actively. In doing this, you show that you're really paying attention, rather than thinking of something else, or waiting for your chance to speak.

Last year, I learned a good approach to active listening from Samaritans, a British not-for-profit organisation that provides support for people at risk of suicide and takes 3.6m phone calls a year. The Samaritans approach is to think of listening as a wheel with five spokes.

Silence. This is at the centre of the wheel. It may sound banal, but if you want people to talk, you need to resist the temptation to talk too much yourself. Let them finish. Wait five seconds; if you mentally count to five, you may be surprised by how slowly the time passes. They may start talking again. If they do, wait for them to finish and count to five again. Rinse and repeat. When the person really *has* finished, it's time to help them continue. You have six choices.

Clarifying. If something is vague, invite them to explore it further. Then wait. Remember, it's more important to get things clear for them than clear for you. If you wait, you'll probably find that most things that seemed ambiguous will get clearer.

Open questions. To keep questions open, ask questions that can't be answered with a simple noun or a noun phrase. You're looking for stories and narratives — but avoid starting with why. "Tell me a bit more about x," counts as a question. Then wait.

Reflecting. If you simply reflect back by borrowing a word or a phrase from what your report has said to you, that can often help them get talking again. If your report says a marketing campaign didn't work, and then stops talking, you can say: "So the campaign didn't work." Then wait.

Encouraging. Just simple words like yes, right, OK and go on can help people continue. Then wait.

Reacting. A single sentence like "Wow, that must have been tough," will often elicit more detail or more clarity from them. Then wait.

Summarising. If the person seems to be rambling, saying something like "Let me play back to you what I'm hearing," can help to get them on track. Then wait.

One way to remember the things in the listening wheel: people who use these techniques are SCORERS: Silence, Clarifying, Open questions, Reflecting, Encouraging, Reacting, Summarising.

JONAS, THE CEO whose question triggered this discussion, found that once he used the techniques of the listening wheel, the members of his team giving those 'short and to the point' answers began to open up, and the information fog around what they're doing cleared. That's a great improvement. Now the problem is how to move those meetings forward so the person doing the reporting learns something and goes away with some clear actions. The answer to that, too, lies in asking good questions.

This is a perfect opportunity for startup CEOs and managers to apply some coaching skills. But some tweaks are needed to the classic techniques that come from life coaching, since OOOs between CEOs and their reports are different from meetings with a life coach. For one thing, the context is clearly business: it's about improving the operating and financial performance of a company. Increasing happiness or self-esteem is a side-effect, not a primary goal. And for another thing, the coach in this context (ie the CEO) may well have a deep understanding of the nuts and bolts of the problem that's being discussed — deeper, maybe, than the manager being coached.

I've helped some CEOs evolve a list of questions to run through. The list borrows from techniques described in two terrific coaching books: Michael Bungay Stanier's *Coaching Habit*, and Nancy Cline's *Time to Think*. Here's how it goes.

The Focus Question

Once your report gets comfortable talking freely, the issue is how to stop them — or more precisely, how to get them to home in on what's going to be relevant and actionable for them. A simple way to do this is to ask: "What's the challenge for you here?" You may need to come back two or three times to get that turned into something specific enough to work on. But the result is that you'll both get a clear sense of the goal, and what would constitute a good outcome.

The Blocking Question

You'll naturally move on to discussing possible options for what to do, and keep prodding for more, but often your report will only see a few ways. That's often because they're assuming something that blocks them from seeing alternatives: facts about the world, possible facts about the world that they think are true but may not be, or convictions about themselves or the world that are firmly held but probably not right. The single most valuable thing you can do for someone who's stuck in this way is to put that assumption on the table so they can see it. "What are you assuming here that's blocking you?" Again, you may have to ask a few times before they see it.

The Incisive Question

If your report can replace that blocking assumption with a more realistic one, that can suddenly open up new possibilities. That's why it's so incisive to ask: "If that assumption turns out to be wrong, what new options will become available?" You may need to be more explicit by figuring out the precise opposite to the blocking assumption, and articulate that.

The Helpful Question

Stanier calls it the 'lazy' question, but most people in companies don't want their bosses to relax on a lounger by the pool while they're choking in the water and sinking. It's absolutely your job as a CEO to ask "How can I help?" — but note the word. It's not "How can I do it instead of you?". You're playing your part as an advisor, supporter and helper, but they still have agency. It's still their job to get it done.

The Trade-Off Question

When you remove a blocking assumption, the solution to a problem at work often comes from realising that something that you thought had to be done can in fact be safely ignored or postponed. But you need to make that explicit. Otherwise, your report may go away enthused, but reduce their chances of success by still trying to do everything they'd planned to do. Hence the question: "What must you give up or say no to if you're going to follow this new approach?"

ASKING THESE FIVE questions is a great way to get one of your reports to find a new solution to a problem. They've learned something. And to wrap up, you need to get them to commit to:

- What they're going to do
- When they're going to do it
- How you will know they've succeeded.

How to plan six months of effective one-on-ones

ALINA FOUNDED A startup that has raised $10m, and she's now responsible for a team approaching 50 people. She regularly meets the people who report to her, and she's learned to ask great questions. But she still doesn't think she has got it 100% right. "What makes you feel it's not working?" I asked.

"There are long silences," Alina said. "We seem to run out of things to talk about. Frankly, I don't feel that the one-on-ones are helping anyone."

One way of looking at the journey of managing people one on one is to think of there being five levels.

- Level One: Management meets regularly to discuss issues.
- Level Two: You organise one-on-ones (OOOs) with each of your department leaders to more closely investigate the issues unique to a given team.
- Level Three: The OOOs now have a clear process. For instance, the person who reports to you brings updates and an agenda to the meeting, and you share a document with them containing notes, action points and follow-ups for afterwards.
- Level Four: Knowing the five things (see page 120) that good CEOs make sure the people who report to them

are doing, and asking the right questions (page 126) to maximise the effectiveness of your one-on-ones.

ALINA'S PROBLEM IS that she can't get to the next level. Her one-on-ones feel stale. When she started doing OOOs rigorously, there was a backlog of things to discuss between CEO and reports. The structured process of OOOs allowed the backlog to be worked through systematically. Likewise, OOOs with new hires worked well too: there was lots to work on in the first quarter, partly to help them understand what made the company unique and to ensure things were being done the way the founders believed they should be done. But once those things have been achieved, what next?

Sometimes there are things you need to do to fix your existing one-on-ones — starting by looking at what's really going on the relationship between CEO and report. In Alina's case, she described something odd about her OOOs with Jim, her online marketing manager. The cry she'd heard several times from Jim was 'I'm just not getting any guidance' — a strange thing to say during a one-on-one meeting whose very purpose was to give him just that.

What became clear, as we discussed it further, was that Alina felt Jim wasn't showing enough initiative. She couldn't see why he was asking her for support on things which she didn't have much experience in either. Alina's view was straightforward: if you haven't done something before, just do some research (starting with Google), and have a go before you ask for help. Don't worry if it's not perfect, Alina felt; you can improve it later. But Jim wasn't doing that.

The trouble was that Alina had unwittingly revealed this disappointment — so Jim had lost the confidence to ask for her help. We solved the problem together: Alina started probing Jim for the exact details of what he couldn't do, and then simply talked through the tasks with him. She gave him lots of time to come up with options, resisting the temptation to jump in, and gave him answers only if he truly ran out of ideas.

To her surprise, Alina found that Jim did in fact come up with good ideas that he could execute. And the result was that after each one-on-one, Jim felt like a success. With Alina at his side, he'd found solutions to his problems. And this growing confidence allowed him to solve things independently.

LET'S ASSUME YOU'RE there too: you're running one-on-ones with your reports so effectively that they truly want to open up with you about what they're having trouble with, and as a result you're able to help and support them. What next? What happens in OOOs at Level Five?

What I've seen with CEOs who've become experts is that they're able to take down the frequency of their standard one-on-ones from weekly to fortnightly. But they don't simply spend less time with their reports. Instead, they identify a number of other types of update and OOO discussions that are worth having, and use those alternative slots to run through them one by one.

With six different types of discussion, that provides a plan for 12 sessions: weeks 1, 3, 5, 7, 9, and 11 can be classic OOOs, while 2, 4, 6, 8, 10 and 12 can be items chosen from a list of broader topics. Add a week of vacation, and you've filled a 13-week quarter.

The result is that if you're a CEO responsible for managing five people, this template gives you an easy-to-use plan for your next sixty (ie 12 x 5) one-on-ones.

Six types of meetings work well once a quarter, and can be put into the even-numbered weekly slots:

1. *Performance.* Annual reviews of how well people are doing may be fine in large, slow-growing companies where things don't change fast. In a startup that could double its headcount in a year, it makes more sense to do a performance review each quarter.

2. *Relationship.* Separate from how well the person you're managing is doing, there's a question about whether the relationship between you is healthy. It makes sense to block out one meeting each quarter in which both manager and report can give their assessment of the situation, raise questions, and resolve problems.

3. *The big project.* In many startups, senior people often have one thing that matters — they'll succeed in the role if they get it done, and they'll fail if they don't. That shows the value of having a stand-alone meeting to plan or discuss just that project.

4. *Look forward.* When your company is changing fast — growing, pivoting or restructuring — it makes sense to sit

143

down with each person you're responsible for, and discuss what they're likely to be responsible for in the coming six months, and what study, training or support they'll need to get there. That's distinct from a performance review.

5. *Team management.* As your company grows, the people you manage increasingly have to manage others. What management skills do your reports have? How can you help them be more effective?

6. *Quodlibet, or what you will.* Even though your reports already have regular chances to give updates, ask questions and raise concerns, there are lots of things — some of which may be personal — that they may not feel fit easily into the standard meeting structure. It makes sense to give your reports an opportunity once a quarter to have a meeting with you to talk about whatever they like. You need to signal the significance of this: it's a chance for them to prepare and reflect together on a big issue that might normally be out of scope. People who think their managers care about them personally tend to rate them highly. An unexpected and deep conversation about something they value can have a transformative effect on how they think of you.

LOOKING AT THE types of discussions you can include in a structure of one-on-ones, you may be tempted to wonder why to bother. After all, you've got lots of other calls on your time, so why spend any more time than you need to with the people who report to you? Wouldn't it be better to get on with stuff you're working on yourself, like fundraising or strategy?

Two thoughts may help you here. One is that as CEO, you are responsible for the performance of your entire team. Although your investors may make sympathetic noises if you tell them sales are down because your VP sales needs to be replaced, they know that the most effective CEOs coach their management team so well that this problem rarely arises. It's a lot cheaper to help someone raise their game from good to great than to fire them and get someone else.

The other is that many CEOs find they get lots of interruptions from their team each day. The more you can use one-on-ones to make sure that you and each person who reports to you have a shared understanding on all the important issues, the fewer interruptions you'll get. So paradoxically, spending more time on OOOs can *save* you time.

ONE LAST THOUGHT: What do you do if you realise, after a number of sessions with one of your reports, that actually they're just not capable of applying the SCRIM framework to their own team? If so, they're not going to be able to ensure that the people reporting to them are appropriately selected, coached, reliable, involved and monitored.

If that's the case, and you've done your level best to help and encourage them over a period of time, then you've learned something important: that one of you isn't actually the right person for the job. Either you're not cut out to be CEO, or they're not capable of managing the team they run. And the problem therefore is yours to fix.

FUNDRAISING

How to start fundraising

IN A RECENT webinar, where I was helping two dozen CEOs with the wide range of challenges facing them as they grow their business, about half the questions that came in beforehand were about just one topic: fundraising. At first sight, that may seem bizarre. Are these guys obsessed with money? What about their product? Their team? Their customers? Or the half-dozen other areas on the agenda?

Reflecting further, I realised that if you think of a startup as a machine, then those other things are important engineering issues to make the machine run faster or more smoothly. You can address them from time to time like you would take a car in for a service. But fundraising is different: money is fuel, and if you run out then you cannot move forward at all. So it's not surprising how much fundraising looms in the minds of startup CEOs.

I've seen startup fundraising from the perspectives of founder, investor, board director and coach.Reflecting on what I've seen, here are the top four fundraising mistakes that CEOs often make when they set out to fundraise.

1. *Making the wrong decision about intermediaries.*

Here's an email that I send, in various forms, about twenty times a year:

> Dear John, Here's the thing. At the early stage where we invest, it's all about the founders. And founders have a big advantage if they're good at researching who to approach, building compelling slide decks and plans, and making a persuasive pitch to investors. We've recently done some analysis on which companies that reached out to us for funding were most likely to be the ones we invested in, and we found that the companies whose founders couldn't fundraise by themselves and needed advisers or boutique investment banks like yours to do it for them were in the bottom slice. So for now, we've decided to just not look at anything that comes in via paid intermediaries like you. Sorry! — Tim.
>
> PS: Please take us off your mailing list.

So at seed stage, where we invest, it's rarely worth using professional intermediaries when you're raising money. But things change as the company grows. One investment banker I know recently took on as a client a fast-growing tech company that had great difficulty raising its previous round. When the job came in, the banker had his junior people do the necessary work to put together a private placement memorandum (PPM) and a slide deck, and to ensure the company had all the information needed for due diligence in an online data room. He then made precisely six phone calls to potential investors he knew had history investing in the geography, the stage and the sector. Three weeks later, the company had commitments for a raise of between $50 and $100m. The valuation at which

149

the money came in, after a few auction rounds, was more than twice the highest initial offer. "Easiest $2m I ever made," the banker told me.

The banker's delight at how effortlessly he earned his fee might tempt you into thinking that this means the company should have raised by themselves. But in fact, it's the opposite. As a CEO, you need to assess whether an intermediary can help you raise money more easily and quickly, since effort and delay take you away from the job of running and building your business. Then you need to assess what the cost of using the intermediary will be — or indeed whether there will be a cost at all, since in this case the valuation that the banker achieved by triggering competition between the investors was so much higher than what it would have obtained by itself that the effective fee was heavily negative.

So this is the first question you need to ask before you start fundraising: does it make sense to use an intermediary? Let's make the criteria more precise. If you're early stage, or if the decision is qualitative rather than quantitative, or if the targets aren't used to dealing with bankers, or if you can readily name a number of potential investors, the answer will probably be no. Otherwise, you should use an intermediary and save yourself a bundle of work and grief. You can jump to the next chapter, since the bankers will do the rest for you.

2.   *Loading the funnel with too few potential investors.* For all their reputation as evil geniuses, many venture capitalists allow weirdly subjective factors to influence their investment decisions, some of which they're aware of but

many of which they're not. Did they like the shirt you were wearing? What colour was your slide deck? Is your product aimed at people like them or their kids? How successful was their firm's last deal? How happy or depressed are they feeling today? How well are they getting on with their partners or their spouse? What did they have for breakfast, and how long ago? What was their most serious mistake in the past year or the past week?

In your personal life, if you want to find a good partner and protect yourself from randomness, it's a good idea to go on lots of dates. When running a startup, it's a good idea to reach out to lots of investors.

The banker's list of six perfect investors that I described above is a dream scenario. A better approach is to think of your fundraising as like selling B2B SAAS: you need to think about the successive stage that a successful 'customer' will need to pass through in order to sign the deal and send the money, then make a guess at the conversion rate from each stage to the next. Multiply the percentages together, and you'll get a number showing what percentage of the people you reach out to will send you a term sheet.

For instance, suppose your five stages are:
- Send them an email
- Have a phone call
- Meet in person
- They visit your office
- You pitch to their partners

If you expect half of the prospects to drop out at each stage,

151

then your overall conversion rate will be 50% x 50% x 50% x 50% x 50%, which is 0.5^5, or just over 3%. This means that you'll need to talk to more than 30 people to get one term sheet. So if you want to have three term sheets, that would mean reaching out to 90 potential investors.

Note: that doesn't mean spamming 90 random VC firms you found on some publicly shared Google sheet. It means doing the research to find 90 investors who are visibly interested in your stage, geography and sector, and who don't have stakes in your competitors, and then reaching out to them with a personal, not visibly canned, approach.

3. *Failing to qualify prospects.* Many investors think the best response to an approach from a company they're not interested in investing in is to do nothing — simply to ignore it. That's dispiriting for startup founders, and especially dispiriting for first-time founders who make basic mistakes in their initial approach to investors, and hence get a low hit rate. The result is that founders are often so grateful, so pathetically grateful, to get a response from anyone that when an investor emails them back, they'll drop everything and cross town (or sometimes even hop on a plane) to go see this exciting potential source of cash.

Whoa — not so fast. Before you invest significant time and emotional energy in the relationship, it makes sense to verify that there's a reasonable prospect of closing a deal. In B2B sales, a common checklist is BANT: does the potential buyer have the *budget* to buy your product, do they have the *authority* to make a decision, do they recognise they *need* it, and does their *timeline* match your needs?

I've developed an investor checklist that startup founders can use when fundraising, whose purpose is to help you screen out the VCs, family offices, strategic investors and angels who aren't likely to close. It goes by the acronym FACKWITS; see page page 156.

4. *Misunderstanding how serious investors are.* Your best friend calls you to say they went on an amazing date. They had a delightful evening. Maybe they kissed, maybe not; nice people don't tell. But at some point in the evening, you're told, the other person looked into your friend's eyes and said, "I *like* you." Surely, your friend asks, it's time to book the venue for the wedding?

You'd probably try to dampen your friend's expectations. One date, however enthralling, doesn't guarantee that the couple are destined to have a blissful sixty-year marriage with four children and a white picket fence. There are lots of steps and obstacles to go through before the wedding can take place, let alone their lives afterwards.

As with life, so with venture funding. VCs have a process for making investments. Some have mapped it out in explicit stages in a CRM, with consciously chosen conversion criteria at each stage of the funnel that I described in #2 above. For others, the process may be much more impressionistic and intuitive. But what professionals have in common is that they have limited resource for looking at potential investments, and they try to focus those resources on the deals that are most likely to come to fruition. That's the reason for term sheets; no point spending $25,000 on a full set of legal documents only to discover that there's fundamental disagreement on one of the basic terms.

Talking to VCs about funding is incremental, and you need to be realistic. The degree of enthusiasm that a given investor shows for your business is likely to be more related to their temperament and personality than to how likely they are to invest.

Things may seem like they're getting serious when you start talking to a partner rather than an associate. (To be clear, the 'GPs', or 'general partners', are the people who raised the fund and make the decisions. The LPs, or 'limited partners', are the pension funds and foundations who actually put up the money that the firm invests. And some firms like Andreessen Horowitz, confusingly, call all their staff *partner*.)

Since VC firms don't want to waste time on deals that are unlikely to happen, it's a sign that things are getting serious when they're willing to come to your office. That is a sign that a conversation with you is worth more than a journey of twenty steps from their desk to their conference room: now they're willing to invest in a journey across town, some travel time, and a $20 Uber.

And the deal is progressing further still when you're invited to meet multiple partners. Sometimes you'll be asked to pitch the firm's regular partner meeting, and they'll make a decision the same day on whether to offer you money. The most flattering thing is a combination of the two: an office visit where multiple partners come. (If the entire partnership flies in to see you, then the balance of power has flipped; they're pitching for the privilege of giving you money, and trying to convince you that they'll be more helpful than the other top firms they fear you're talking to.)

Finally, there's the term sheet. The whole point of a term sheet, as I've explained, is to get all the deal points clear before switching on the taximeter of lawyers' bills. It takes half an hour or less for a VC to generate a term sheet and send it to you, but it's a sign of concrete commitment. Although term sheets typically say explicitly that they're subject to commercial due diligence, and they're not binding except for the bits about confidentiality and who will pay whose fees if the deal falls apart, most US firms send a term sheet only when they've firmly agreed to do a deal on exactly those terms. The only thing that will derail it is if they discover your murder conviction or the fact that half the emails on your customer list are billg@microsoft.com. Some Europeans are more weaselly about this; one London-based VC I know has a habit of agreeing term sheets and then 'finding' issues in the due diligence that require a modest tweak in their favour, like a 70% cut in valuation or an option to invest the same money at the same price next year. But the difference between 'still talking' and a term sheet is still vast.

AS A STARTUP founder you need to block your ears to what investors are saying, and observe what they're doing. Six people who 'want to learn more' is a lot better than nobody taking your calls. But two funds who've had second meetings, three who've visited, and one who's sent you a term sheet: that's a more concrete measure of the progress you're making.

How to qualify an investor

"I DON'T UNDERSTAND what's going on," said Gunther. "I'm spending so much time talking to investors, I barely have any time left to run my company. I'm going to meetings, taking phone calls, rushing from one café to the next, and responding to dozens and dozens of email inquiries and requests for documents. Yet the fundraising isn't any further ahead than it was two months ago. They're all still interested. But all they do is ask for more information. What a load of f***wits."

Gunther is one of the CEOs I coach. He's bright, and his business is interesting and growing, though not as fast as he'd like. Once we started digging into his investor problem, it became clear that there were several things going wrong. None of the investors felt any sense of urgency, so nobody was in a hurry to move things forward. Gunther himself didn't have a clear idea of what the process ought to look like. But the most important problem was that much of his time was being spent talking to investors who, frankly, weren't going to close — because for all his confidence, Gunther was too bashful to qualify his investors.

That shortcoming is forgivable, since there's often a power dynamic when an entrepreneur goes to meet a VC. Investors often feel it's their right to interrogate you about your business, but get sniffy if you start asking them questions. But a couple of gentle inquiries in an email, a bit of research into their portfolio, and another two or three questions in the smalltalk section of a first meeting can often help you figure out how much effort it's worth devoting to them. That's why I'd suggest adopting the fundraising equivalent of the BANT checklist used in enterprise sales.

Let's call it FACKWITS.

Do they have Funding *available?* At any given moment, about one in eight VC firms have finished investing one fund and are in the process of raising the next. An unknown number of private investors or family offices are waiting for a 'liquidity event' to produce money before they will be ready to make their next investment. It's so obvious that it's banal, but if you want to close your round in the next ninety days, then people who don't have money right now aren't going to take part in it. If you're delicate, you can probe for this.

Are they Actively *investing?* Even family offices and angel investors with plenty of cash on hand can spend time meeting companies just to learn about the industry or just to keep up to date. While they might invest if they come across something astounding, it's not a good sign if they can't tell you how many new investments they made in the past six months or how many they plan to make in the coming year.

Can they Commit Knowledgeably *to the timeline?* Everyone spends some time trying to understand your business before they come to a decision. For a PE firm, that might be 100 work hours; for a VC, more like ten; for an angel, maybe two or three; for a crowdfunding investor, just the six minutes it takes to watch your video and fill out a form. If they're going to lead the deal — setting the terms, taking a board seat, exercising the rights of everyone who commit money alongside them — then they will need time to produce a term sheet. If they're following someone else's money, they'll need time to review *their* term sheet, and then either read the final investment docs or (if they're an angel investor) find a lawyer to look at them. Someone who's about to go on a two-month vacation, get divorced or start a new job as CEO of an investment bank isn't likely to have that time. If you try to hurry them along later in the process, they may then drop out, spreading FUD and wreaking havoc among the other investors. So you need to discuss in detail early on what their investment process is, what due diligence they'll need to do, and how ready their lawyers are, so that they can commit to a timeline but be fully informed before they do so.

Where *do they invest?* Dumb question, obviously, but while some investors are truly global, and happy to wire money to people they've never met and receive updates only by email, others follow the principle of Arthur Rock, the VC who gave Intel its seed funding and also invested in Apple. A hundred years ago, when I was writing a book about Intel, Rock told me that he had a firm rule never to invest in a company more than forty minutes' drive from his house in Silicon Valley. You can figure out which type any given investor is by looking at their portfolio. An investor who's in scope on the other criteria but is geographically constrained may not reveal this, but they may therefore be an unlikely prospect for you. They may be taking the meeting because they're considering making their first investment further afield (or they may be researching an investment in one of your competitors closer to home).

Are you in the right Industry? At Walking Ventures, we like SAAS, platforms, marketplaces and tools. We don't invest in hardware, e-commerce or gaming. To avoid wasting every-one's time, we publish these choices on our website. Not all investors do the same; those who haven't developed an invest-ment thesis yet may *want* to see lots of pitch decks and busi-ness plans in order to decide their strategy. If you're talking to an investor who's never backed a company in your space or remotely close to it, you may be contributing to their educa-tion rather than raising money.

Are you asking for the right Ticket? The 'ticket' is the amount that a VC invests from their own resources — as in "We do tickets of $3–5m, in rounds of $5–10m" — and it's important to be aware that no matter how much they like you, professionals who are deploying money on behalf of institu-tions usually have a defined set of deal criteria. If your ask is outside their range, either way too small or way too high, the deal won't happen. And talking to them is a waste of breath.

Is your company at the right Stage? This differs from ticket size, because the amount of money that makes an investor the lead in one round will make them at best a follower in the next. Many VCs are willing to do a smaller ticket one round earlier than their typical sweet spot in order to see how the company performs, so that they'll have an advantage over other funds when it comes to the serious investment they hope to make. This means your business may still be at the right stage, even if it doesn't superficially look like it. But if an investor typically wants to see $3m in annual recurring revenue (ARR), and you're at $500K, then your meeting with them isn't likely to lead to money any time soon.

NOTE THAT THERE'S a difference between being qualified and being interested. It may well be that the fund you're talking to is absolutely ready and willing to make an investment in the space, but doesn't rate you as CEO or doesn't think your company has performed well enough. But it's necessary: when an investor fails, it's best to move on to others.

Checklist in hand, Gunther soon began to find he was regaining control over his time, since he was able to identify the least likely prospects and politely end the dialogue with them. But what do you do if you take a meeting with an angel or VC, and you disqualify them ten minutes into the discussion? If you've crossed town to see them, it's tempting to get annoyed and dismiss them as, well, fackwits. But that would be a mistake.

Remember that the startup world is an ecosystem, and that if you do helpful things for other people, those helpful things are likely to come back to you over the long term even if not over the short. So at the point you realise this guy is never going to give you money, switch gears. Stop selling your business, and try to figure out how you could make the meeting useful. If you make it useful for them, they'll remember your generosity.

You can learn something useful from every person you meet, and investors are no exception. At the gear-change moment, try to say this to yourself: One of the many things this person knows is an insight that could be hugely valuable for me, but they don't know which insight that is. It's my job to find out.

Don't forget that every meeting with an investor is free pitch practice. Observe which things you said seemed to pique their interest. Observe where they got bored. Note what seemed impressive or disappointing. Note which questions they asked. (It's much easier to do this if two of you go, and one watches reactions while the other talks. Even if you're resource-constrained as most startups are, it can be valuable to hunt in pairs for the first few meetings.) Since you'll make mistakes while practising, it's much better to make those mistakes on investors where there was little chance of getting their money anyway than on your best prospects.

Finally, remember that you can ask investors for help, even (and sometimes especially) if they're not going to invest. Who else should I speak to? What advice would you give me on the business? What mistakes do you think we could be making? What risks do we need to prepare more for? If you can resist the temptation to fill your allotted time with a selling pitch, you can ask their advice on these things. Hence the saying that if you want money, ask for advice; if you want advice, ask for money.

The first half of this is the clever reverse-psychology piece:

investors are so jaded by the hundreds of entrepreneurs they meet every year who are trying to get a share of the pile of loot they control that it's refreshing (and flattering) to hear from a founder who seems to love them for their wisdom rather than their cheque-book. This is rare, and VCs sometimes find that it's the best founders who do this, and they consequently offer to invest unprompted.

The second half of the aphorism is a point of clarity. When an investor refuses your request for funding, they'll sometimes tell you why, and occasionally in detail. Write down their reasons carefully; they're gold dust. Although many investors are individually wrong, the crowd is more often right. If you start hearing the same messages from lots of investors, it's time to have a serious think about whether you might be wrong and they might be right. I cover this in more detail on page 235.

How to close a funding round

YOU'RE CEO OF a fast-growing startup, and you're in the middle of a fundraising round. You've carefully considered whether you should raise the money yourself or use a professional intermediary. You've made sure to reach out to enough potential investors early on. You've qualified those investors to make sure they're not wasting your time. And you're aware of the signals and behavioural signs that indicate that the VCs you're talking to are serious and moving forward at an appropriate pace. To sum up, your pipeline is appropriately full and it's progressing at the right speed. What could go wrong?

I've observed that startup CEOs often assume that once they have investors who say they're committed to taking part in a financing, they assume that they're home and dry. But they're often wrong. There are three important things that can go wrong, and they're worth watching out for.

1. *You forget to manage cash during your fundraising.* I know a talented founder who built a good startup in the travel industry, and negotiated an attractive exit to a big company whose name you'd know. The terms were agreed, the paperwork was prepared, and the transaction was due to close on 23rd December. Then the startup CEO's phone rang. It was the VP he'd been negotiating with at BigCo, the company that

was going to buy her startup. Unfortunately, the VP explained, BigCo had discovered a problem — and sadly, wasn't going to be able do the deal on these terms. The startup founder was stunned: all that time and effort, and the transaction was going to abort? "We can still complete the transaction," said the VP. "It's just that the price is going to have to be 40% lower."

What was the deal-breaking problem the buyer had discovered? Well, it wasn't really a problem as such — only that the buyer had noticed that the startup was running out of cash. That meant that the startup's BATNA had disappeared. Rather than having a Best Alternative To A Negotiated Agreement (the idea, from negotiation theory, of the most advantageous course of action if the talks didn't succeed), the startup had left itself in a position where if the deal collapsed, it couldn't make its monthly payroll. It would be forced to shut down operations within two days if the deal didn't close. Someone at BigCo had realised that the deal no longer had to be attractive. It just had to be *better* than the seller's BATNA of shutting down. And the buyer took advantage of this at the last minute, by giving the price a savage haircut.

Another founder, the CEO of a professional marketplace, started the fundraising process with eight months of cash. She hoped the negotiations will be done in six, so the company would have a two-month buffer to get it done. But she liked having a plan B, so she raisedd a chunk of debt. The money came from an existing investor, who received a high interest rate, plus a bunch of warrants, *plus* an arrangement fee. It was a high-return deal for the lender, who was given a fixed and floating charge over the company's assets — meaning that if the company couldn't pay back the money when it fell due, then the lender would own the business. But this debt deal, expensive though it seemed, had the following effect. As the potential investors moved further into the process, they examined the company's financials, and they saw that there was no urgency on the sell side about the deal.

When you think of it in those terms, it doesn't seem complicated. The lesson is straightforward: manage your cash so that during the fundraising, and for a good buffer of time afterwards, you're solvent. Most VCs aren't evil people; they wouldn't knowingly try to take advantage in this way. But those who might be tempted to get the company into exclusivity, slow down the process a little, and watch the CEO squirm as the business slides towards insolvency, now know that strategy won't work. You want to be able to wait out your potential investors if you have to.

2.   *You give your investors unpleasant surprises during the due diligence.* It's a cliché that greed and fear are among the 'animal spirits' that the economist John Maynard Keynes identified in the behaviour of investors. VCs, like buyers of public equities, switch back and forth between the two: desperate one day not to miss out on a 'hot' deal that some other investors they're jealous of are doing, and terrified the next day of looking like an idiot for having backed a terrible company. But one difference between a VC deal and a public-equity investment is that stock prices on the NASDAQ or the NYSE change every few seconds as new information comes in. Elon Musk casually tweets that he's thinking of taking Tesla private

at a well-chosen price of $420 a share? Great; the company's worth more. Buy, buy, buy. Oh, the funding isn't secured after all? Quick, sell.

When a VC invests in your company, by contrast, they're locked in for years. This makes sense, and the general partners of funds build their businesses around this expectation: they make their own investors commit to a ten-year partnership, usually with a couple of extensions in case they haven't had time to exit from all their deals by the time the partnership has to wind up. So you'd expect the short-term vicissitudes of your company's fortunes wouldn't make much difference on such a long-term investment.

But you'd be wrong — and the VCs' rollercoaster journey back and forth between greed and fear is especially agonising during the weeks between the day you shake hands on the price and the day the money hits the bank.

Since venture deals are mostly about the promise of the future, even things that might not seem like deal-breakers to you can rapidly cause a VC to lose enthusiasm. Those little nuggets of bad news — a team member quitting, a big client backing out — don't just make them look bad to their partners in their Monday meetings. They also might indicate that you're a bad manager, that you don't know your own business, or — worst of all — that you're in the habit of making promises you can't fulfil.

The lesson is this: as you start the process, and as you look at what's in your slides, pay careful attention to what predictions you're making that could come to fruition during the period of negotiations, and make sure that you're unshakably sure you can deliver on them. That way, you never have to give your proposed new business partner an unpleasant surprise. And, they won't need to share your disappointment, and you won't have to deal with the fallout.

Better still, keep some *good* news in reserve. I've seen some CEOs skate quite close to deliberately pre-arranging positive surprises, where they're able to use small pieces of good news as an excuse to move the conversation forward. It's not great to have to email an investor to say "Hey, you said you were going to get us a term sheet by Monday; it's now Thursday. We're pretty desperate — when are you going to send it over?". Much better is to write: "Hi, just thought you might like to know we closed the month with $10,000 more revenue than forecast. BTW, we've had an offer in from another fund, but we'd love to work with you as investors. Would you like a bit more time to get that term sheet over to us?"

3. *You try to use logic to negotiate the valuation and terms.* A while back, I was having dinner with the general partners of half a dozen VC firms, and we were talking about the difference between our internal revenue forecasts and the competing forecasts that the companies send us. "It's a kind of battle of the spreadsheets," said one VC, "a digital trial by combat." "I've been amazed," said another, "how much I've changed my mind about the potential market size after looking at the CEO's bottom-up estimates." A third replied: "Yeah, and we just closed a deal at a 30% higher figure than we first offered, all because the founders convinced us we were using the wrong discount rate in valuing the cashflows."

Actually, I made that story up. It's not true. I've never heard a serious VC investor admit to having changed the price they're willing to pay based on new information from the company about market size, or on superior analysis of forecast financial performance that they were given by the company. To oversimplify: a better spreadsheet will *never* increase your valuation.

It's usually possible to get VC investors to move on some of the deal terms if you ask them nicely, as long as your wish-list isn't too long. But on the core issues of the pre-money valuation, the liquidation preference, the anti-dilution rights — the big items that clearly affect the economics of the deal — there's only one thing guaranteed to get VC investors to improve their terms: competition. If they're convinced there's another credible investor willing to pay more, and that you're seriously considering doing the deal with the other guy, that can prompt a second offer. It may be covered up with the fig-leaf of the investor listening carefully to your valuation arguments, but that's usually a matter of professional pride: nobody likes to admit that they're being pushed around.

If you're a risk-taker, then it might be tempting to follow the strategy described by Ben Horowitz in his book *The Hard Thing About Hard Things*, and simply bluff (ie pretend you have an offer that doesn't actually exist). But bear in mind two things if you do. First, VCs talk to each other. It's dangerous for founders to tell investor A that investor B is further ahead in the process, or more firmly committed, than they really are, especially if you made the mistake of telling them who investor B actually is. It only takes a text or a two-minute call between them for your credibility to plunge to earth in flames.

And second, even if you're sure there's no way for the VC to test the credentials of their phantom competitor (the equivalent of a shill in an auction or a find-the-lady con game), you're taking a risk the investor will realise that they're being played.

Some investors (and I'm one of them) recognise that it's a form of cognitive distortion to allow the price someone else is willing to pay for an asset to influence the price they should pay. People who try to resist this distortion therefore won't budge when you threaten them with the competing offer, whether or not it exists. You might think that if they're so super-rational and quantitative, then you have nothing to lose by trying the bluff and then if it fails coming back to them and accept their price after all. But that's not always how things work out. You've demonstrated a behaviour that they may find unappealing, and they may decide not to give you money on those grounds. That's why it's much better to try to get several simultaneous, competing offers.

SOME FINAL WORDS about the fundraising process. This year I've seen two different companies run into problems when fundraising, because they allowed their *existing* investors to decide what valuation to ask for. They named that valuation to all the potential new investors who invited them in for meetings, only to find that the new investors separately (and rapidly) withdrew, complaining that the price was too high.

Some founders get into the same position almost by mistake. Knowing there's an advantage in negotiation to getting the other guy to name a price first, they try to parry valuation questions by saying something like "We don't know yet; we're going to see what signals we get from the market". But the VC brushes off that response and pushes for a number. Under pressure, the founder names a price that's too high.

The VCs you're meeting will have seen hundreds of companies this year, if not low thousands, and will have had the chance to compare the valuations all those companies were asking (and the final price at which deals actually got done) against lots of detailed metrics, including their growth rate, their unit economics, and the size of their target market. To put it another way, the VCs are surprisingly often in a better position than you to know the fair value of your business.

They're not going to tell you that value: that would require too much honesty. But you could be wildly wrong if you base your valuation on what you read last week about some other company in a related space in TechCrunch, or what your markup your board directors hope to get on their investment in your last round.

This is particularly problematic at the first professional funding round. As amateurs, angel investors are less well-informed than VCs: that's partly why they mostly make worse returns. They're also less price-sensitive. So it's galling for them to learn, only after working with you for a year or two, that the price they paid for their shares was too high, and that as a result their paper profits are going to be a lot lower than the percentage increase in your sales.

WHICH BRINGS US to a fundamental truth about fundraising. Founders spend a lot of time agonising over the details of how they pitch to investors. What clothes should I wear? How many slides should I put in the deck? What fonts should I use? How confident should I seem during the meetings? How long should I wait before I follow up with investors? And so on. Yet in one sense, all these activities are like agonising over lipstick colours for your pig.

The fundamentals of your business — how good your product is, how much your customers like and use it, how much evidence they've given of willingness to pay for it, how profitable it is, how fast you're growing: all these things are real, and all of them have a profound effect on your future. It's *these* things that will ultimately determine whether VCs or others are willing to give you money. And if you focus on them, you're unlikely to go far wrong.

How to run a startup that's running out of cash

"I NEED HELP," said James. "My startup has got cash to last us seven months, but we've got a load of liabilities like leases and employee notice periods. If we can't raise a new funding round, we'll need to start winding up four months from now. And if I tell the team they may be out of a job, it's going to kill morale, and I won't be able to hire people into the two open positions we urgently need filled. I want to go out on the road to talk to new investors right now, but my existing investors won't let me. They say the business isn't far enough forward to raise a new round yet. What should I do?"

James's dilemma will be familiar to many startup founders. And it's tempting to jump into action, like he wanted to. Yet James's first idea on what to do — put together a slide deck and immediately start trying to land meetings with investors — will distract him from running the company, which in turn will reduce the chances of keeping it alive and raising more money. In other words, it's exactly the wrong thing to do. So what should you do if you're in James's position?

First, adjust for what behavioural economists call availability bias. The vast majority of stories on TechCrunch and other startup news sites are about businesses that are doing really well — that's why they sought the publicity in the first place. But those businesses aren't a fair sample of all startups: the reality is, for every TechCrunch success story, tens of thousands are struggling to deliver growth and cheaply acquire and maintain customers.

LET'S BE HONEST: most companies miss their targets. If your investors are less experienced, like angels or family offices who expect the startups they invest in to be as predictable as McKinsey or Goldman, that will be a problem.

That said, even seasoned investors know that missing multiple targets in a startup can have a compounding effect. Slower user growth, higher customer-acquisition cost, higher churn, and lower customer lifetime value will combine to shorten — sometimes dramatically — the company's runway. The cash your model said would last 18 months suddenly looks like it's going to last only 12, or even 10.

The tempting thing to do is just keep plugging away. You avoid looking at the financial forecast you shared with your investors before your last round, in the hope that they won't think about it either. If they do, then you draw on your reserves of optimism to come up with good reasons why you'll catch up. But that catch-up is much harder than it looks. If you've forecast 10% growth for six months, that compounds to a 77% increase in sales over the period. If you delivered a more modest 5% a month for five months, then you're 27% bigger — and only a miracle will raise your sales by 50% in a single month and get you back on track. Conclusion: you need to do something *different* from what you've been doing since you raised money.

I've seen many founders in this situation. Some deal with it badly. Here are the six key strategies that I've seen from those who deal with it best.

1. *Focus on the metrics.* At the beginning, most founders raise money on a tiny number of early users, a prototype, or even 'a deck and a dream'. They convince early-stage investors that they're smart and energetic enough to have a reasonable chance of success, and the investors take a punt on that basis. But as the business matures, so do the investors. Professional investors at seed or Series A are looking for real evidence that you have the potential to build something big and profitable. So they pay a lot of attention to customer acquisition cost (CAC), churn, and lifetime value (LTV). If the numbers just aren't there, they'll pass — either by simply saying no, or (to keep their options open) telling you they love you and the business, but 'it's a bit early'. (That's an understandable strategy, since who knows? You might turn it around, and they want you to call them if you do.)

What this means is that these metrics are absolutely vital to the long-term survival of your business, and have first claim on your attention. Your top priority is to test some changes that will boost them. When startup founders talk about how much 'runway' they have left, they usually think in terms of months — but a better way to think about runway is in terms of how many more *attempts* do they have to get it right.

If you can carry out four experiments a month in each area instead of one, then you've got four times as many rolls of the dice to get it right. So come up with good tests that will uncover the insights you'll need to fix things, and then put those insights into effect.

2. *Reach out to investors — sparingly.* This isn't a ban on speaking to investors, merely on spending too much time on them. There are plenty of things you can do to make sure potential backers know who you are. You can speak at conferences. You can send them email updates. You can meet them over drinks. But don't let anyone start a due diligence process that's likely to lead to disappointment, and don't start sharing lots of detail about stuff that isn't working yet.

In the past, VC firms typically were made up of a handful of partners and an assistant. The huge increase in assets under management (AUM) in the venture-capital industry means that these days firms are under pressure to use a reasonable chunk of the 2%-a-year management fees on running their fund rather than on yachts and planes. So they hire lots of associates and analysts, and set them the task of getting to know all the startups they can and trying to get early access to promising deals.

So when you come off a half-hour call with someone from a VC firm, you might feel that it was a big success because you got on well, and you think they're excited about investing. That's not how the call went from their end: you were talking to an associate who just added one record to their CRM, and collected five data points about the business, which gets them towards their target of covering 30 new startups this week. Has it materially changed the chance their firm will invest in you? Maybe. Maybe not.

It makes sense to qualify both the seniority and interest of VCs you're talking to, and to limit your time accordingly. But you can go further: use the calls to get their advice. That doesn't just flatter the investor, and give you a preview of how valuable they might be if they invested; it can help you check your assumptions, and gives you a clearer idea of what you'd need to achieve to get their money.

3. *Maintain your enthusiasm in front of the team.* Remember that your job as founder is like the job of the captain of a damaged warship in the year 1810, two thousand miles from port. (For more details, see Patrick O'Brian's brilliant novel, *Desolation Island*) Your chances of crossing the ocean safely before you run out of food and water are slim, but you're the captain: you don't share that info with the crew. Your mission is to stay positive, to chart a course for the nearest port, and to inspire the crew to fix the broken mast and sew up the sails. The advantage of running a startup rather than a vessel in mid-ocean is that you can share your worries and fears with your lover or your coach. But not with your colleagues.

4. *Manage costs.* Continuing the seafaring analogy, captains of commercial sailing ships had a simple strategy when they were being chased by pirates. If the pirates looked like they were getting close enough to board the ship — and kill or enslave everyone aboard — you started throwing things overboard in order to speed up your own ship: first the water, which you can replace at the next port. Then the cargo, which

is after all only money. Then the cannon, if you can't win a pitched battle and just need to run. Think similarly for your startup: identify what you *must* have in order to survive to the next round, and jettison everything else. Now is not the time to be making investments that will pay off in five years.

5. *Get your investors to bridge.* Behavioural economics demonstrates two other useful things that can be helpful to you: loss aversion, and the endowment effect. Loss aversion, first identified by Amos Tversky and Daniel Kahnemann, means that people care more about not losing $100 than about winning $100. And the endowment effect means they value stuff they already own (ie shares in your company) more than stuff they don't own (like new investments they haven't made yet).

The way to frame the story to your investors is that there's a great opportunity, but it'll be lost if you run out of cash. That can help persuade your investors to provide bridge financing, even if they didn't originally intend to. (That's why people call them backers: you go back to them, and back to them, and back to them...) The message has to be: things aren't right yet, but here's a convincing plan for how I can fix them in *x* months. And if I achieve that, then here's why the company will look like a great opportunity for new investors, and will be worth a lot more money than it is now.

6. *Privately prepare a Plan B, but don't yet activate it.* The most valuable thing you can learn from the next-round investors that you do speak to is the metrics they'd need to

see to be enthusiastic about giving you money. What growth rate, what customer-acquisition cost, what payback period? Then take a long, hard look at your plan. It could be that today's numbers are simply too far away and not changing fast enough for it to be even half-plausible that you'll get there in time, even after you've thrown the drinking water overboard.

If that's the case, then you need a plan B.

You may not like the sound of the hard decisions you'll have to take, but remember that failing to take those decisions is tantamount to taking the decision to shut the business down — or even worse, simply run out of cash and trigger an insolvent liquidation. If you leave the taxman, creditors, and even employees unpaid, then the resulting mess may spoil your chances of getting backing for another business, and you also risk breaking the law.

Don't let that happen just to avoid asking yourself the hardest of hard questions. You might get a second shot by making radical changes: losing all the sales and marketing people, cutting back to a skeleton crew to work on the product, pivoting to something else. That strategy can often result in taking out 80% of your costs, which can turn a three-month runway into a year or more. And given how many companies have created something new by pivoting from their existing business — like Twitter — the opportunity to test something else could have a high option value.

But at this stage, you don't need to commit to choosing your plan B. You simply need to know what it is, and to have decided a date, and a set of numbers, on which to make your decision. If you don't hit the numbers on that date, then you make the change.

NONE OF THESE things is easy, I know. They take effort and self-discipline, but they're often the route to a successful outcome. And if you know what they are in advance, they can help a lot.

BOARD SKILLS

How not to get fired
as a startup CEO

ONE OF THE biggest worries of startup CEOs with the least experience — up there with the fear of telling people their great idea without an NDA, or giving away any equity at all in their companies — is that they'll get fired by their venture-capital investors.

That worry is mostly misplaced. For many VCs, the ideal investment is one where the founder is so good at the job that they can continue, Zuckerberg-like, all the way from their dorm room to $100 billion. They know that's not going to happen with half their founders, but to borrow the old saying from advertising, they don't know which half. Each investment is therefore a triumph of hope over experience.

I've only ever met one VC who talked cheerfully about 'swapping out' CEOs from her portfolio companies. But a founder-CEO isn't a fungible component in an engine, like a gasket. A better analogy is that if your startup is your baby, then the founder is its mother. Nobody who 'swaps out' a baby's mother expects things just to carry on as normal.

What happens when a board fires a CEO

Firing a founder-CEO is a messy, expensive business. First, it takes a while for the VC to realise that the company's failure to make progress is down to its leadership, and to figure out that the leader has to go. Then, over the next few months, the VC tries to get across this message to the founder-CEO: your shareholding in the company is your most valuable financial asset, so it's in your own interests to have that asset effectively managed. And then, if the founder-CEO still doesn't get it, the VC pulls out the investment agreement a few months later and figures out the process by which the board or the investors can kick out the founder. Then finally, after lots more anguished conference calls among the investors, they do it. This process typically takes a year, and of course the company makes no progress during the period — so if it's still alive after you're out, whatever cash it burned during the period is wasted.

Outsiders also forget that the VC who fires the CEO becomes subject to what the political commentator Tom Friedman called the 'Pottery Barn rule' in connection with George Bush's 2003 invasion of Iraq: *You break it, you own it*. It's not easy to recruit a new leader for a loss-making startup that has lost its way — good CEOs typically want to join companies that are succeeding, not struggling. And although some VCs have been known to take on the job themselves temporarily, that's even less appealing than running a CEO search. While a good minority of VCs used to be company founders themselves, most of them find the job of being a general partner less stressful, more rewarding, and easier. In their more honest movements, many VCs would probably also admit that they couldn't do it anymore. People like Dharmash Mistry, who founded Blow, a home beautician service, after being a partner at Balderton and before joining Lakestar, are among the honourable exceptions to the rule.

The result, contrary to what many people outside the industry think, is that VCs are generally reluctant to fire company founders who don't perform. And when it's clear that they need to act, they're slow to do it. It's like the comment attributed to Winston Churchill about the USA's late entrance to World War II: "The Americans can always be counted on to do the right thing — after trying everything else first."

SO WHAT IS it that really gets CEOs pushed out from their own startups? Well, the fastest route to getting fired — legally speaking — is to commit a 'repudiatory breach' of your employment contract, meaning something so terrible that it immediately and irreparably damages the company's faith in you. That could include committing a serious criminal offence unrelated to your work. Or harassing an employee. Or inappropriate sexual behaviour, or discrimination.

Yet there are plenty of CEOs who have done all of these things and stayed in the job. I know of two separate startup founders who awarded themselves generous salary increases without taking the trouble to ask the board — something that's unequivocally forbidden in most standard VC deals. One of them is still in the job four years later; the other got fired, but not for that.

Incompetent plus dishonest?

My standard answer to founders who wanted to know the circumstances under which I'd support firing a CEO was that I'd never consider it unless they were both incompetent and dishonest. Yet in practice, even that is often not enough: since incompetent people sometimes lie to cover up their failings, it's surprisingly common that when companies run into trouble, the board discovers belatedly that the numbers they've been given have been massaged. Investors realise that this behaviour is partly a response (though a pretty poor one) to the high pressure of running a startup. When someone who pleads not guilty of a crime is convicted, the court doesn't usually start a new trial for perjury just because they lied in their unsuccessful attempt to get off.

Even CEOs who are more broadly dishonest as well as incompetent can survive for a surprisingly long time. The interesting thing about the saying that "you can fool all the people some of the time and some of the people all the time, but you can't fool all the people all the time" isn't the third part; it's the first part. Most of us start by assuming that other people we deal with are broadly honest. And that gives the unscrupulous a period of default goodwill in which they can fool us — a period that is much longer than you might expect.

The toxic cocktail

What I've observed over the past five years, though, is there's one toxic mixture that has a high chance of leading to the dismissal of a CEO — and it's the cocktail of incompetence plus really poor investor relations. Here's how this applies to CEO-founders.

Most VCs, like most founders, are honestly doing their best for the companies they invest in. They want to help and be supportive. They introduce the CEO to people who run other portfolio companies. They invite them to retreats and offsites. They recommend coaches. They find consultants, headhunters, non-execs and EAs. Some VCs have a stable of staff and consultants to help their startups, all free of charge.

VCs may be investors, but they're also people just like you and me, and people expect relationships to be two-way. It's not unreasonable for them to hope that you'll (a) recognise their attempts to help, even if unsuccessfully; (b) show them you value their effort; (c) take their contribution seriously and consider it carefully; and (d) either act on it or show your reasons why you don't intend to.

Fail to engage with your investors in this way, and you're taking on sole responsibility for the fortunes of the business. And once you've done that, you've turned a company problem into a personal problem.

So what do you need to do to get fired? Here's a breakdown of the common behaviours I've seen in situations where a CEO ws removed by their board.

1. *Show you're incompetent.* Miss your targets by a mile. Poor results in the business are necessary, but not sufficient, to indicate incompetence. There can be plenty of other reasons why the outcome isn't what everyone hoped for — ranging from product to people, and from changes in the external landscape to mistakes made at the outset. Only when there's seriously disappointing results with no obvious other explanation does the focus turn to the CEO.

2. *Have no data, or ever-changing data.* The one data

point nobody can run away from is the cash your company has in the bank, and that's hard to avoid. But it's hard to know what's going wrong if the rest of your data is unavailable or unreliable. Running a startup without data is like driving a car without a dashboard. Repeated changes in reporting tools for finance and software development are also a bad sign.

3. *Have no plan, or an ever-changing plan.* Not many founders and CEOs are so out of it that they truly have nothing to say when asked what they're going to do. More often, the evidence of no plan is that at every board meeting, whatever initiative was promised last time has now been superseded by a bigger or better idea, and the initiative from the meeting before that has been simply forgotten.

4. *Fail to follow up or complete.* Poor CEOs start initiatives but don't finish them. They make commitments and don't keep them. They agree to do things, and then fail to.

5. *Blame the world.* When things aren't going well, good CEOs look inside first, and ask themselves what they could do better. With weak CEOs, it's often the world that's at fault. Over time, their investors figure out that simple bad luck is unlikely to be an adequate explanation.

6. *Keep saying it's OK when your VCs know it's not.* It doesn't take a genius to check how much money you have in the bank and compare that with the past and the plan. If there's a serious mismatch, then coming to board meetings quarter after quarter with upbeat tales about how wonderfully

everything is going will fool your lazier investors for a while (especially if they don't take the trouble to compare board packs with each other). But not forever.

7.   *Hide information or mislead them.* If you've had some major bad news and you're wondering whether to reveal it to your VCs, then pause to reconsider: by withholding the information, you're taking a step towards your own demise. Investors often acquire a sixth sense for when things aren't going well, and it's connected with seeing how you interact with your team. Not many people are great liars; when a VP of sales or engineering is asked to give a more upbeat account of how things are going than is justified by the facts, they're not always successful. Once your investors realise they've been actively misled, then you've passed an important stage.

8.   *Resist their efforts to find out what's going on.* When everything's going well, the busy VC will largely leave you to get on with it. Questions between board meetings – and approaches to people in your team — may indicate their concern. If you push back, you can stop then getting what they were looking for, but you won't be dealing with their concern.

9.   *Complain about the burden of their info requests.* It's true that some investors — especially those that haven't actually run startups themselves — try to cover up their inability to contribute anything to the company by asking lots of questions, sometimes those that create a disproportionate burden in gathering and analysing information. A good rule of thumb is to ask what the company would do differently based on the

answers it finds. If the answer is nothing, then there can be a case for diplomatically raising that with the VC (preferably not at the board meeting itself). But some pieces of analysis are to your product or your sales strategy what a whetstone is to an axe: they help you work much, much more efficiently. If your reaction to this kind of information request is to push back or claim you're too busy chopping down the trees to sharpen the axe, then you're padddling towards the waterfall.

10. *Turn away their introductions (or ignore them).* Something that many VCs can do quite well is to know people who can help you, or who know how to do things that you don't know. Some investors are too prolific with their intros, and you may need to filter them for likely value before committing time to them. But refusing even a 15-minute call with an offered connection doesn't play well.

11. *Dismiss their suggestions and ideas.* One advantage that VCs almost always have over the CEOs of the startups they invest in is perspective: they may know more about what's going on in the startup ecosystem, because they're seeing new deals every day. And they may know more about what can go well or go badly in startups, because they've seen dozens when you've seen only one, two or three. Some VCs are like some CEOs: they have ten ideas a minute, of which nine are useless. Seasoned founders do two things with suggestions: they consider them (and show that they've done so), and then decide how much time to invest in investigating them. CEOs who lose the confidence of their boards tend to be those with a standard response when someone on the board raises an

idea: they jump in, barely drawing breath, to explain why it's a stupid idea, has been tried before, or both.

IF YOU'RE A startup founder-CEO, I'm sure that you've never exhibited any of these behaviours, and that's great. You're not in danger. But it's always valuable to know about the behaviours of those *other* CEOs who get replaced in their companies, and what might have caused them to lose the confidence of their investors. Forewarned is forearmed.

How to get on with the Vcs on your board

AT FIRST IT looked like it was going so well. Gavin had circulated a stylish, informative deck two days before the board meeting. His investors showed up on time. They read the materials. And they looked pleased with the great progress being reported. Yet when the meeting ended three hours later, Gavin felt like he'd been put through the mangle. His product, his reports, his sales processes, his team, his hiring: everything seemed bad. "Before I went in," he told me, "I'd have rated our execution an 8.5 out of 10. After, it felt like a 4."

What went wrong? As Gavin's CEO coach, it was my mission to find out. The superficial answer was obvious: the investors had asked some searching questions, and had concluded that things weren't going as well as Gavin thought. And it was the VCs' fiduciary duty to the shareholders — not to mention to the limited partners in their own funds, whose money they were investing — to pull the alarm cord. One of the board members, thinking of himself as a fearless truth-teller, had even talked Gavin through some quick mental arithmetic. In three heartrending minutes, he proved elegantly that the current trends in customers and revenue simply wouldn't allow the company to raise another round by the time it ran out of cash.

There was a deeper issue at stake here. A smart and persistent entrepreneur with great qualifications and an impressive CV, Gavin had been working sixty hours a week for the past year without vacations. Not surprisingly, he reacted strongly — and negatively — to what the investors told him. Although he rationalised it in professional terms, Gavin felt like any parent would feel if you observed that their baby was ugly.

After the meeting, Gavin sent an email to the board, thanking two of his investors for being so helpful. His pointed silence about the mental-arithmetic whiz was deafening. It took some time to talk Gavin off the ledge of saying or doing something that would be catastrophic to the relationship with his VCs.

THIS PROBLEM IS more common than many of us admit. The tech industry has a long tradition of believing it healthy to tell the unvarnished truth. At Intel under Andy Grove, they called it 'creative confrontation'. Some Intel employees thought it was the best way to run a business; others would run out of the room in tears, or quit. Walter Isaacson's fascinating biography of Steve Jobs showed the Apple CEO could be scathing to his reports. And even today, VC Ben Horowitz cites with approval the behaviours that exemplify a wartime CEO who gets stuff done in difficult times: "uses profanity purposefully...is completely intolerant, rarely speaks in a normal time...neither indulges consensus-building nor tolerates disagreements".

Which is perhaps why some investors prefer to market themselves as 'entrepreneur-friendly' . But this can invisibly slide into choosing not to push back even when that is what's needed. At one board meeting, I observed a successful VC smiling and nodding reassuringly, but asking no questions. After the meeting, in private, he described the team's execution as 'total shit'. And when I asked him why he hadn't told them frankly what he thought, he had a clear answer: "I can't meaningfully influence the outcome," he said. "When this business fails, the founders aren't going to blame me for not warning them — they'll blame the the the market or the competition. And they'll recommend me to other founders as a good VC."

But surely there's a happy medium between investors who humiliate their CEOs and those who wave supportively to them as they approach the cliff. What I've observed as an investor and board member is that the approach described by Kim Scott as 'radical candor' is a great start.

Radical candor when you're a VC means (a) caring personally for the founders, but also (b) challenging them directly. If you do (a) but not (b), that's 'ruinous empathy'. If you do (b) but not (a), it's 'obnoxious aggression'.

But knowing this in principle isn't enough. What does it require in a board context? Effective VCs exhibit a number of common behaviours; if you're a CEO, you might consider sharing this list with your board before your next meeting.

1. *Start by acknowledging successes.* You may feel it's too cheesy to follow the approach recommended in Nancy Kline's Time to Think book (at Amazon in the US and UK) of beginning every meeting with a formal session celebrating what's going well. But there are plenty of ways to do this more

discreetly. Note that a piece of *Harvard Business Review* research showed that top-performing teams typically give nearly six positive comments for every negative one.

2. *It's 'we', not 'you'.* Unless you've signed a weirdo invest-ment agreement, you have the same interests in the company's success as the founders — so act like it. Behave as if you're on the same team, and trying to solve problems together. Not like an examiner testing students who didn't do their homework.

3. *Ask how you can help.* CEOs learn over time that advice and ideas are currency as debased as the Venezuelan bolivar: they're in such common supply that they're not worth much. The commodity that is far more scarce is execution. So rather than adding something to a founder's to-do list, try crossing something off it. That earns ten times the kudos.

4. *When trying to diagnose problems, use 'how', not 'why'.* The why makes it too easy to sound accusatory, and often comes with an unspoken side order of 'you moron'. Learning how is often the better way to understand context.

5. *Finally, avoid evaluating founders at the board.* One of an investor's' most important jobs is to give CEOs feedback on how they are doing. But this is best done one on one. It's worst done in a conference room where others are present and there's a long agenda to get through. Use the board meetings for governance and strategy.

BUT IT'S NOT just investors who can up their game. How can you reduce the risk of clash if you're a founder?

1. *Remember your investors' needs.* That may sound weird given that they're the ones with the money (and the experience, as they'll often tell you). But VCs have challenges of their own: they need to show their partners that they made a good decision to back you, and they need their portfolio to show good performance so they can raise another fund from their limited partners If they're frustrated or angry, it's probably not because they've written you off. It may be because they know your company could be doing great things, but you're not there yet. And despite their air of omniscience, your VCs are human beings too with their own failings and inadequacies — one of which may be not knowing how to give feedback in an encouraging way.

2. *Hunt for action items.* If it feels like your investors are piling on the criticism at a board meeting, then try saying this: This is super-helpful input. How do I turn it into something I can do in the next 30 days with the resources I have? That can help reset the conversation from coulda-shoulda to what's actionable now. If their answer isn't clear or realistic, probe.

3. *Then write down their recommendations, and read them back to your investors to confirm you've understood.* This makes sure you come away from the meeting with a realistic to-do list. If it looks too daunting, you can also ask them to estimate what time and resource would be required, and

calibrate that against what you have available before agreeing to it.

4. *Deploy their perspective.* The greatest advantage investors clearly have over you is that they see inside lots and lots of companies. Even if you're a serial entrepreneur with two, three or four startups under your belt, they see hundreds or thousands of pitches each year, and they're likely to have stakes in 20, 50 or 100 businesses, where they've seen many ways in which things can go well and things can go badly. Ask them: What have you seen other companies do in our situation? Are there any CEOs you've backed that you think could help me with this?

5. *Above all, seek their input on funding.* The one thing VCs know from their own gut, is what your company needs to have in place to attract a next round of investment. If, like most startups, your business has chosen the path of losing money in order to grow faster, then the single most important thing you need to do is to ensure that by the time you run out of cash, you've made enough progress to convince investors to give you more. As a coach, I often encourage founders to keep updating their forecast of where they'll be in sales, product, engagement and so on by their cash-out date, and to verify regularly whether this will make them an attractive investment prospect three to four months before the deadline. Board meetings are an ideal forum for this reality check — and if your VCs' hunch is that you're not on track to be able to raise, then listen carefully and take their concerns seriously.

Both sides need to be realistic about what they can expect from each other. As a VC, you can't expect the CEO magically to acquire skills they didn't have when you invested: unless you're willing to make a major commitment to them outside board meetings, you'll need outside help if you want them to sharpen their game. If you are a CEO, you can't expect your VCs to solve your problems for you: they can be a great sounding-board, and they can introduce you to people. But it's you who will make the business succeed, not them.

How to negotiate your own salary with a board

YOU HAD TO hand it to Donald: his timing was impeccable. His startup had grown quickly to over 200 people, and top-line sales were running at four times the level of the year before.

There were some problems, too. They were losing money on each sale. As a result, the company needed to raise more money — something that Donald did almost effortlessly, using a mixture of charm and bullying to persuade the investors to reach into their pockets for another funding round.

And that's when Donald struck. No sooner was the money from the bridge round in the bank than Donald went back to his board. "I've had a job offer," he explained. "The strategy consultancy where I used to work would like me back, and they've come up with pretty attractive terms. I'd love to stay and help build the business, but the balance of risk and reward needs to be right. If I'm going to stay, I'll need a 50% salary increase."

THE INVESTORS WERE over a barrel. Without anyone committed to running the business as CEO, the cash they'd just put in would be swiftly burned, and there would be little chance of raising a next round. Much though they hated to admit it, keeping Donald was worth more — a lot more — than the extra salary that he was asking.

Donald had just given a textbook demonstration of three important things CEOs at venture-backed businesses should do when negotiating their salaries with their board. Let's look at them one by one.

1. *Choose the right moment.* No matter how you get on with your investors, the negotiation of your salary as CEO is a zero-sum game: every extra penny in salary is a penny from the investors' pockets. If the company is loss-making, as most startups are, it also brings forward the date when you will need new financing. So pop the question when you're in the best position to negotiate.

2. *Have a clear BATNA.* When two sides in a negotiation can't come to a deal, it's often because the two sides don't have a clear enough view of what each other's alternatives are if they can't agree. Your BATNA, according to Roger Fisher and William Ury's book *Getting to Yes*, is your 'best alternative to a negotiated agreement'. A stronger BATNA makes it easier to walk away from the negotiation. If your implied threat is that you might possibly update your CV job, then your board may not be terrified. They may feel that's a risk worth taking, and postpone discussing your package for a few months. If your plan B is to accept a contract to start a highly-paid job elsewhere starting Monday, then things are different.

3. *Demonstrate value.* Founders are understandably emotional about their companies. Investors are much less so. Whatever you may feel about the loyalty you've shown over

the years, the late nights you put in without overtime, the family time or the vacations you missed, venture capitalists and angel investors are rarely minded to reward you for past performance. This is true even if your past compensation for that performance feels like a pittance. Rather, it's best to make your case in terms of the future, explaining why the increase you're demanding will deliver value to investors.

That can be an upbeat message — if I stay, we'll have a billion-dollar exit — but it can also be downbeat. Helping investors avoid a catastrophe is worth something too.

DONALD GOT ALL of these things right. Yet three weeks later, he'd been unceremoniously fired. Unpicking the story reveals some other issues that he failed to pay attention to.

4. *Check that your proposal will seem fair to the other side.* Contrary to what you might think from reading on the web, my experience across many boards and many companies has been that for the most part, VC investors try to act fairly. What's more, they want others to treat them fairly too. And if your definition of the right moment is when you have your business partners over a barrel, that's something they will remember — and resent.

You might expect them to act like rational economic agents, and simply calculate the likely outcome to them of plan A, where you stay, versus plan B where you leave, and pick the one with the higher expected value. But many VCs will want to signal to other founders that sleazy behaviour isn't rewarded, or simply get emotional. They may be willing to take some pain in return for punishing you.

That's exactly what happened in Donald's case, because he forgot to apply the reality check of whether his proposal would seem fair to *them*. Once they received his ultimatum, the board simply held a conference call between them and then decided to offer the job to Jamie, his COO, Modest, reasonable and honest. Jamie now runs the business, and he's doing pretty well at it. Donald, by contrast, ran into a problem with that consulting job he presented as his BATNA. He tried a little too hard to talk up the terms of the new job, and the result was that it fell through. When I last checked LinkedIn, he had a startup that had been 'in stealth mode' for a suspiciously long time.

By contrast, investors will appreciate frankness with them about your personal circumstances. If you're having trouble meeting rent or mortgage payments, or have an elderly parent or a toddler to support, then that's highly relevant information to share. If money worries make it hard for you to focus on the business, then they should know.

Reflecting on CEO salary negotiations that have had successful outcomes and left both sides feeling content, I've identified a few other common themes.

5. *Propose a fair mix of jam today and jam tomorrow.* Self-evidently, if you found a startup that succeeds, you're likely to make a great deal of money. The rewards aren't dissimilar to winning the lottery, except in the case of really successful startups like Amazon or Facebook, whose founders

have so much cash that they could give someone else a lottery win every week for a decade.

In thriving startup ecosystems, there are plenty of investors willing to provide the capital to founders who can provide the labour — the ideas, the talent, the hard work. But founders can't lay claim to a gigantic free option. In return for the upside on top of whatever they had in their previous job, it's reasonable for founders to take some salary sacrifice in return.

Twenty years ago, many investors took a tough line: they liked startups where founders started out paying themselves low or minimum wage or, if founders had money of their own, the proverbial \$1 a year. Thankfully, times have changed: VCs now realise that running a startup is a stressful job, and that being paid nothing or near-nothing while seeing your bank balance shrink every month makes it even more stressful. That's why investors who seek long-term value for their companies want founders to be fairly paid. But they still like to see a little sacrifice.

Lots of things influence how big that sacrifice should be: how strong the business model is, how big the market, how much the founder was earning before. But investors don't want you to be chilled out about whether your business succeeds or fails.They want you to trade, as Lewis Carroll's White Queen might have put it, some jam today for jam tomorrow.

6.   *Use comps with care.* Consistent with the weight they put on fairness, most VC investors will be influenced by arguments about what's common elsewhere in your industry. If you can provide 'comps', for instance evidence that local startup

founders comparable for stage and sector get 30% more than you, that will go a long way to getting the outcome you want.

7. *Understand the dilution effect.* If you raise $2m for a startup and pay yourself $200,000 a year, then self-evidently you're transferring 10% of the raise straight back to yourself — and doing so in a way that is highly tax-inefficient, since the income taxes and employment taxes you and the company will pay on your salary and cash bonuses are much higher in most jurisdictions than the capital-gains tax you will likely pay on the increase in the value of your shares on a successful exit.

But there's a more important point. Suppose the company does well enough to raise money 18 months later at three times the valuation. Had you been able to scrape by on a mere $100,000 salary, the money saved could have reduced the number of shares that had to be issued in the first round. And thanks to the 3x step-up in valuation, the equity that would have been left in the company could now have been sold for $300,000.

This is probably the most important point to consider when you're an early-stage founder. Particularly in the first couple of years, the rate of return you can achieve on an early salary sacrifice could be immense. And an open conversation about this with your investors can be helpful. Not everything about the negotiation needs to be zero-sum.

8. *Remember that this is different from team compensation.* For most startup founders, your potential reward if the business succeeds is an order of magnitude bigger than your

most senior hires, and two or three orders bigger than the rest of the team. That's why your compensation should be handled differently from theirs.

How honest to be with your board

I'VE ASKED THIS question to a lot of startup founders, and most of them think the answer is obvious. The trouble is, their answers disagree. Some say honesty is the best policy, all the time. Others follow the view of Lucy Kellaway, the in-house professional cynic of the *Financial Times*, who argues in a witty column that there are four lies every CEO *must* tell.

Lucy's advice may work well for CEOs of big public companies, but it has perils if you run a startup. When you compare venture capitalists on the boards of private companies with institutional investors on the boards of public companies, the VCs usually have more ownership, more power, more inside knowledge, and more perspective.

Unless you believe you are smarter than all your investors put together, there's a high risk of being found out if you are dishonest — especially when you remember the old saying attributed (tenuously) to Abraham Lincoln:

> You can fool all the people some of the time and some of the people all the time, but you can't fool all the people all the time.

The consequences of dishonesty are serious, too. In both startups and public companies, a well-drafted CEO contract will usually include a list of things that constitute 'cause' in the

US or 'repudiatory breach' in Britain. These are equivalent to what hospitals call *never events*, like leaving a scalpel inside a patient's abdomen, or amputating the wrong leg. If you get caught doing one of them, you're liable to be fired immediately and without notice or compensation.

That's bad enough in a public company, where a CEO may have a few million dollars at risk. In a startup, the consequences of a repudiatory breach can, paradoxically, be a lot worse. This is because the founders' shares represent a far higher proportion of their rewards than in mature businesses, and many startups have 'reverse vesting' provisions on the those shares.

The primary purpose of reverse vesting is to make founders who depart from the company leave behind a proportion of their shares — initially 100%, lessover time. This is reasonable, since a loss-making nascent business is going to be almost worthless without anyone to run it. Only over a period of a few years does it acquire the resilience to survive a founder's departure.

But reverse-vesting agreements are also to 'hold your feet to the fire', ie to give you an extremely powerful incentive not to misbehave. The typical arrangement is that if you're fired for cause *at any time* during the reverse vesting, then you lose not only your unvested shares but all your shares. That $100 dinner with your partner inappropriately charged to your company expenses could prove to be the most expensive meal of your life. So the stakes are high.

The more subtle issue is how to behave when talking to your board about your company's current situation and its prospects. There are two risks.

One is that you're too downbeat. If you do this, you'll be following the lead of Cassandra, the ancient Greek heroine to whom the gods gave the gift of foresight, plus the matching curse that other people would never believe her dire predictions.

The other risk is that you're too upbeat, like Pollyanna, the hero of a 1913 novel, who was so relentless optimistic that she found reasons to be positive even after losing the use of both legs.

WHETHER AS INVESTOR, board director or CEO coach, I've seen both extremes. One CEO was a Pollyanna who ran a high-ticket marketplace business, where transformative partnership deals were always 'about to happen' but never quite did, and where the CAC ratio looked great because her metrics silently assumed (without any evidence) that every customer who spent $50,000 would come back and do the same again every year for the next four years. Pollyanna fooled most of the board for a year, but got fired in the end.

Cassandra did better: she preached doom so often that her board meetings were a succession of pleasant surprises, where the predicted disasters were always less bad than expected. And there *were* plenty of disasters. She admitted to the board she'd hired the wrong CTO. On their advice, she fired the entire tech team and got the product built more cheaply by an agency. Then a key partner whose blessing was essential to the success of the project pulled out at the last minute. That problem was too big to fix. She called an emergency board

meeting, and suggested winding up the business and returning the remaining cash to investors.

Yet all these apparent disasters turned out to her credit. Her
two biggest investors — who both lost money on the company
— were so impressed by her honesty that they offered to back
her next startup, sight unseen.

Perhaps there's some reverse psychology to be aware of
here. Many VC investors are smart and original people, who
never want to take things at face value. So when a Pollyanna
comes along declaring that everything's going gangbusters,
they look for problems. And at the board meetings led by a
Cassandra, they look for reasons why things are *better* than
they seem.

Across 50-odd investments, I've seen that founders who
are more honest with their boards generally outperform those
that are less honest. I've also seen three things that successful
founders always tell investors, and three things they never tell
them. Here's the list.

1.   *Always tell board members the most important news.*
However clever and diligent they are, investors are unlikely to
have time to know more about your company and your market
than you. That puts the burden on you as a CEO to make
sure your board knows promptly about important things. If
a technical outage harms your relationship with clients, or
a competitor makes a mouth-watering acquisition offer, tell
your board now, not next month. It doesn't go well when they
find out from elsewhere.

2.   *Always tell them your biggest challenges.* By temperament, startup founders have to be optimists — otherwise, why would they be crazy enough to think that a new company could disrupt an entire industry and become enormous? But that optimism can easily slip into a habit of delivering only good news, to reassure investors that they made the right decision by backing you. This makes board meetings useless, since it gives directors nothing to help you with. If you honestly reveal your biggest problems, you'll get free consultancy from two or more smart, experienced people.

3.   *Always tell them about serious mistakes and setback.* Years ago, when I was running an e-commerce business, we had such a nightmare managing our logistics that from time to time I'd ask everyone in the company to down tools, and pack boxes or answer customer-service emails in order to clear our backlog. One day, a newspaper wrote up the story of an angry customer whose shipment had suffered a succession of woes. At the next board meeting, our biggest investor duly gave me a roasting. At the time, I felt hurt and wrongly accused. But with hindsight, it was my fault: I had assumed he knew how much trouble we were having building a smooth operation, but I hadn't actually alerted the board in detail that we were struggling. There's a general moral here: if you ever wake at night worrying what might happen if your board finds out about a problem in your business, tell them about it the next morning.

BUT THERE ARE also things you should never tell your board.

1.   *Never tell your board that you're thinking of giving up.* When you're a CEO, you are like the captain of a ship — it's your job, among other things, to set the direction and inspire the crew. That goes for your investors too; you should acknowledge your difficulties, but always work on the assumption that you will find a way through them, and focus the discussions at board meetings on *how*. If you do decide to give up, though, it's your moral obligation to tell them immediately. You'll then be able to have a useful discussion about your options: whether to hire someone else to run the business, leaving you with some equity in it; whether to return the remaining capital to investors; whether to pivot; or whether to try to for an acquihire.

2.   *Never tell one board member that you dislike another board member.* Investors who sit on boards can sometimes be aggressive and unhelpful, and if things are left unaddressed they can make your life a misery. But when you have a board member of this kind, don't try to make another director your punchbag or your intermediary. This can destroy your relationship with both. It can also makes the entire board opaque and dysfunctional.

Painful though it is, it's better to deal with the issue at source. One of the best entrepreneurs I've backed went to one of his VCs, took a deep breath, and said this: "I know you're doing your best, but we're not getting on well, and I don't think you're the right director for my company. Could you please get one of your partners to take the board seat instead?". The VC was astonished, angry, and then embarrassed. But he agreed.

3. *Never share your cofounder woes with your board.* Talking to your board members about your cofounder is like talking to your mother-in-law about your spouse When cofounders aren't getting on, the first step should be to speak to each other — to be frank about the discontents, and to have an honest discussion about how to fix them. Sometimes, they may not be fixable. But one founder I've coached did exactly this with her cofounder, telling him calmly but directly that she had lost confidence in his ability to lead the business as CEO, and why. Surprisingly, the CEO agreed that she should take over, and they successfully presented the board with the decision as a done deal.

IT'S NOT EASY to apply these observations in your own company. The items on the 'always-tell' can seem hard to confess. Maybe you can't find the words, or don't know how to structure the discussion, or what to ask your board members for. And the 'never-tell' list presents a temptation in the other direction. If you get on with your board members, and you've known them a while, it can be tempting to say something that can never be unsaid.

That's partly why many CEOs work with a coach: an independent third party, contractually bound to confidentiality, whose job is to support you and who has enough understanding of the context and the industry to help you predict how your investors will react.

But there are alternatives. You can reach out to another CEO, preferably one whose company is either at the same stage as yours or a bit further on. Or, if you have a patient and understanding spouse, partner or parent, you can talk to them.

Whomever you choose, you're likely to find the best way through your difficulties by following two simple principles: don't tell lies, and ask for help when you can.

FOCUSING ON WHAT'S IMPORTANT

How one big thing can lengthen your attention span

"TIM, I BADLY need your help," said Lionel. "I've been observing for the past week, and things are much worse than I realised. It's actually down to ten minutes."

The story that emerged from our coaching session was this. Lionel runs a highly successful venture fund (I work with VCs, as well as CEOs). He has a strong team, and a load of investments in hot startups. He's also got lots on his plate. New deals to look for. Portfolio companies to help. Exits to organise via IPOs and trade sales. And finally, the VCs' most important task that portfolio CEOs never see: raising the next fund from their investors.

The result is that like any of his CEOs, Lionel has varied calls on his time from different sources, and lots of projects which he's trying to move forward at any one time, each of which involves a different team of people. And to the outside world, he's pretty good at it. His rapport with founders is strong, his judgment impeccable, and his ability to switch swiftly from one thing to another astounding. It's only from inside that things look less impressive

Lionel's repeated task-switching isn't just something he can do. It's something he can't resist. After gathering data for a week, keeping brief notes on the tasks he's worked on, Lionel has realised that he is unable to spend more than ten minutes at a time on any one thing.

"The effects are disastrous," he told me. "I can't read a board pack without distraction. I can't pay attention in a meeting without checking email or social media. I have no time to read, no time to write, no time to think."

I could understand how he felt, because I'd had the same experience. Four years ago, I was running a seed fund with investments in lots of companies, running around town between board meetings and pitches, coffees with CEOs and conference calls with bankers. And although those activities all seemed productive in their little details, I still had a sneaking feeling that I wasn't, at a high level, actually getting anything done. Not anything that mattered. I wanted to change this, but I felt powerless.

THE PROBLEM WAS rooted in two things. First, I had a deep but unspoken conviction that busy was good — that the more I crammed into each day, the more efficient I was at eliminating the 'dead time' between meetings or activities, the better. And second, that I was a champion multitasker.

It was only once I was able to dispel these two illusions that things started to get better. Truly creative work — 'deep work' as Professor Cal Newport calls it — requires time and space. It can't be boxed into fifteen minutes between this videocall and that team meeting. And multitasking is mostly an illusion: humans are not multiple-core microprocessors that can operate truly simultaneously. Instead, we simply switch quickly, like a single-core processor, between the two tasks we're working on, to create an appearance of doing both at the same time. But it's only an appearance: each time we switch tasks, there's a cost in neurons just as there is with silicon.

If this sounds like something you've experienced, you're not alone. Startups and venture funds are highly complex environments with multiple calls on the time of the people who manage them. The more intelligent those people are, the more they become accustomed to frequent task-switching, and the more hacks and tricks they develop for reducing the switching cost. But the cost is there all the same, and after a number of years it shows itself as it did with Lionel: you wake up one morning, and suddenly realise that you can't actually focus on anything for more than ten minutes at a time.

The journey back starts with correcting both of those illusions. Once you've given up the busy-is-good belief, you can get some air into your calendar, by turning down a load of things you previously said *yes* to, and being more selective about what you spend your efforts on. That's not easy, but it's a start; it means you now have a little time to play with. And once you've given up the multi-tasking belief, you can come to see it as a good thing, not a bad thing, to concentrate on just one task for a much longer period of time. Your dream life changes from a 'manager's schedule', Paul Graham's notion of seeing your work in one-hour appointments that you fill, to a 'maker's schedule', in which "your spirits rise at the thought of having an entire day free to work, with no appointments at all".

But how do you get there? I started by trying the brute-force way: I simply cleared my calendar for a day each week, and then sat down at my desk for a long stretch of uninter-rupted maker time.

Unfortunately, the inspirational muse didn't strike. Realising that I had no plan for the day, I began to feel a slight but rising sense of panic, interrupted with remember-ing things I ought to be doing but had forgotten. I decided to clear my email inbox and knock off a couple of small things. By the time I was done, it was only an hour until lunch, so I made a couple of calls to fill in the time. After lunch, it was back to square one, with once again no plan and no idea how to make good use of the rest of the day. The result was that a month later, I was back to my old schedule. There had to be a better way — an approach to recapturing your attention step by step, with better advanced planning. But it took me a couple of years to find it, and the route came by way of copper. Or rather, COPPER.

APART FROM GOLD or meteorite iron, copper was arguably the first metal that humans put to serious use. It set humans on a path to making useful tools — with techniques like cold working, then annealing, then smelting, and then lost-wax casting — and then into the Bronze Age. So it's a useful analogy for the way to build the tools of focus and attention that will help you be more effective in your work. Think of COPPER as an acronym.

C: Clear your mind, so that you're ready to focus. It's all very well to want to pay attention to one thing for a sustained period, but it's going to be hard to do that if you're hung over, sleep-deprived, over-caffeinated, under-exercised, or anxious. If you want to have a stretch of sustained attention tomorrow, then you need to take action today so that body and mind are ready for the task ahead. Do what's needed to make that your starting point: suitably fed, watered and rested.

O: Organise blocks of time. Make a realistic assessment of how long you think you can concentrate for at a stretch right now. Is it ten minutes, like Lionel? Twenty? Thirty? An hour? Whatever that period is, block out a period that's 25% longer than that — a stretch goal, since you're trying to train yourself. Before you schedule the blocks, make sure there are no fires you might need to fight that could interrupt you.

P: Prepare other people for the change. One of the side-effects of trying to multitask over a long period is that you've unwittingly trained the people you work with — whether it's the team that reports to you, your partners, investors or whomever — to expect swift responses from you. If you're the kind of person who responds to every email within fifteen minutes, then they're not going to be happy if a whole hour goes by without an answer from you. (Pause for a moment to reflect on what signal you've been sending people: you've revealed that you rarely focus on anything for long.) So to make the change, you'll have to reflect on who might need your response or feedback on something, and warn them in advance that you're not going to be available during the block of time you've set aside.

P: Plan how you're going to use the time. It was the lack of a plan that foiled my first attempt at lengthening my attention span: that terrifying, 'free-choice essay' feeling of not knowing where to start. To be kind to yourself, plan in advance, preferably the night before, what you hope to achieve during the time you've blocked out. And to be even kinder, break the task down into pieces — a sequential series of steps that you're going to follow one after another. Write the plan down so you can refer to it as soon as your time block begins.

E: Exercise your attention muscles, but gradually. If you're training to run a marathon, you're not going to start with a target of twenty-six miles on the first day. No: you're more likely to succeed if you follow something more like the 'Couch to 5K' approach, where you start by getting off the couch on day one and taking a short, gentle walk, gradually lengthening that walk over time, then introducing brief periods of running, and then shortening the walking portions until you're comfortably running five kilometres at a stretch. The attention equivalent is to start with that small time block you identified — 25% more than your maximum attention span now — and work really hard to stay on task during that period. Only once you've succeeded should you increase the time a bit. If Lionel sets a 15-minute time block every day for the first week, he can make it 20 the next week, 25 the week after, and 30 in the fourth. Then increasing 10 minutes each week, he can go up to an hour by the seventh week, and increasing 20 minutes a week after that, he can reach two hours by the tenth week. You can tweak the numbers to suit your own situation, based on your attention span today.

R: Restrict the distractions that can contribute to failure. One of the hard things about deep work is that it's hard. You encounter obstacles in the project that you can't immediately solve — and because you're out of practice, your instinct is to switch immediately to another task that's easier and delivers a quicker sense of satisfaction, because that makes you feel you achieved something even if it wasn't what you set out to achieve.

You'll know, better than anyone else, what those procrastination tasks are. Getting your email to inbox zero? Checking social media? Twitter? Phone calls? Snacks? Cigarette or vaping breaks? Once you have identified the distractions, you can change the context to remove them. The method will depend on the distraction: you might disconnect your computer from the Internet, move your phone into another room, put a do-not-disturb sign on your desk, plug your ears into music that blocks out the world without claiming your attention. Whatever: the key thing is to prepare in advance, so that your favourite distractions are out of reach, and it's a little easier for you to focus.

AT THE TIME of writing this, Lionel wasn't finished. But over the space of three months, he had already seen a dramatic improvement in his ability to concentrate and to get stuff done. My own experience was this: after working on this for two years, I was easily able to block out two hours every morning for a sustained, deep period of work on one big thing. It's in my calendar, abbreviated to OBT. And when I set objectives and key results, I take the tasks implied by my OKRs and turn them into a number of things that will take two hours each, and put them separately into the calendar, each in their OBT slot.

If you're a novelist or artist, a joiner or a software engineer, and you can easily lose yourself in a project for an entire day, you won't be impressed. My father, an eminent computer scientist, points out that today's notion of sustained effort looks laughable by the challenges of former times. Take Charles Darwin, he says: he set sail aboard the *Beagle* in 1831, spent nearly five years travelling the world, and then took two years to write up his field journal and travel memoirs in a book. By then, he was already developing his ideas about common ancestors and evolution through natural selection. But it took Darwin *twenty-seven more years* before the theory could be published, with convincing evidence, in *The Origin of the Species* in 1859.

But if you're running a business, then be a little kinder to yourself. Having just one project, one objective, one thing to work on by yourself, is a great deal simpler than managing teams of others and keeping multiple pots on the boil at the same time. So try using COPPER to increase your attention span every day. And don't forget to celebrate, each week, the progress that you make.

How healthy email habits can liberate two hours as day

JEMIMA WAS ONE of the smartest CEOs I'd ever backed. But after sitting on her board for a while, I and her other investors became concerned. The company wasn't going anywhere. Jemima herself was failing to do important things. She ignored introductions or offers. She was stressed, even though she didn't seem to be working a full day.

Here's what I later learned.

• Her reputation for inefficiency came specifically from responding late to email, and sometimes not at all.

• She spent three hours a day on email, partly because she looked at each message several times before replying.

• Her feeling of stress came from knowing that 10% of her inbox mattered a lot, but not knowing which 10%.

• Her inbox contained 11,000 messages — a random mixture of important and unimportant; completed, half-done and not-started; new, known about and forgotten.

NOT MANY INVESTORS would put 'skill at handling email' at the top of the required list of qualities of a successful startup

CEO. Yet email is more important, and has more conse-quences, that it first seems. Email isn't just instant and free. It's also asynchronous: the fact that the sender and recipient never need to be available at the same time means that when email is handled well, it can be your ally, rather than your enemy, in the battle to preserve your attention span and to focus on one thing at a time without interruption. You can use email to exchange information with people around the world ten times faster and ten times easier than phone, and still have the ability to concentrate on deep work. If you can get email right, you don't want to give that up.

But because email has such power, startup CEOs often send and receive lots of it. And it becomes a key channel for communicating with colleagues, clients, suppliers, investors. Get email wrong, as Jemima found, and the effects across your work can be wide and deep.

And this is not something VC investors can typically help their CEOs with. That's perhaps why I got to grapple with the issue fully only when I started working with CEOs as a coach — where I don't own a big chunk of their company and I'm not their best hope to lead their a next funding round. It's simply easier for them to ask a coach than a VC for help on something so personal. As a result, I've had a chance to see a range of problems with email and to see how they can best be solved.

Start with what healthy email habits would look like. You'd read 80% of your inbound mail only once. You'd have 100% clarity on what you've dealt with. You'd respond promptly. You'd have no email stress. And you'd accomplish all these things while reducing, not increasing, the time you spend on email every day.

This is certainly achievable. But if your current email habits feel more like those of Jemima, the CEO I mentioned earlier, then fixing them may seem too daunting — too much like escaping from Alcatraz. That's why you can't do it in one step. You need to plan your escape before you execute it. Here's what I've learned about the best plan.

Start by gathering some basic information. That is, how many mails you get per day, what times and days of the week it arrives, when and how you respond, how long it takes you to respond, and how much you write. I did this a few years using Romain Vialard's Gmail Meter, which emails you a report on the first of the month. (There are plenty of copycats for Gmail/ GSuite, Microsoft and other platform.) This basic information will help you see some changes you can make immediately, like taking yourself off a load of lists, or curing your verbal diarrhea by cutting your messages down to five sentences, and then four or three. Once you've got the data, you can figure out the parameters of how many emails you read and write every day, and how long it takes.

Armed with this knowledge, you can now defragment that time. Say you do email sixty times a day for an average two minutes each time. If you can block out half an hour each in the morning and the afternoon, you may find that the reduced task switching doubles your productivity, and you can get all your email done in an hour. For now, though, all you need to do is schedule a number of slots of *at least 30 minutes* in your diary that total your current time per day.

If your colleagues are used to getting responses from you in five minutes, that means you've been using email as a chat app. You'll need to prepare them for the change, with a polite explanation that you're trying to become more productive. If you like, add this to your email signature.

If you have problems with newsletters, spam and mass emails, then do an unsubscribe blitz. The Gmail functionality that shows 'social', 'promotions', 'updates' and 'forums' in separate tabs from primary mail is helpful here.

If you get lots of internal email, and you're the CEO, then you may be able to cut that by 90% by moving internal communication to another platform. Slack is OK, but less useful than it used to be since the company started trying to drive up hours a day of use. (If you're not the CEO of the business, try to get your company to see the value of reducing the flood of internal cc:s by demonstrating how many inbound cc: messages you get and how much time you could save by handling them more efficiently.)

Turn off all email notifications. If you're doing to deal with email asynchronously, and focus on other stuff without constantly stopping for email, you'll have to stop your computer or your phone interrupting you each time a message comes in.

Use the already available productivity tweaks in your email. In Gmail, enable the 'send and archive' button, which automatically takes threads out of your inbox when you respond. Also, on a computer, use keyboard shortcuts: if your way of sending an email is (a) reach-for-mouse, (b) move-mouse-to-send-button, (c) click send, (d) return-to-keyboard, then switching to a single-click keyboard shortcut will save you a chunk of time. I also make liberal use of 'snippets': canned sentences, paragraphs or entire messages that you can drop into an email to avoid frequently typing the same thing. Gmail has this functionality natively; Streak, a good CRM, does it even better.

Set your email to FIFO. The first-in, first-out approach ensures that when you deal with one message, the next message shown is a newer one, not an older one. This means that from now on, you'll begin with the oldest email in your inbox. And when you've dealt with it, the next one up with be the next oldest. (If you instead do it LIFO, or 'last-in, first-out', the result will be that if you don't finish all outstanding mails in a single session, then next time you come back to deal with email, there will be a small rump of messages to deal with, hidden at the bottom of your inbox, that are now two sessions old rather than one. And it'll get worse.) Also, switch off the preview window in your email, which tempts you irresistibly to look at emails without replying to them.

Tag and move out every message in your inbox. It's tempting to think that you have the willpower and the time to catch up your backlog. But the job will be twice as big as it looks, since half the messages you reply to will generate new email, and your replies to those will generate still more. (See Zeno's dichotomy paradox.) Even if the backlog of mixed-up stuff in your inbox is only a few hundred emails, it's still going to be a depressingly huge job to deal with, which might stop you from acquiring healthy email habits. So, when you're ready to make the big switch, simply move everything out of the inbox except the twenty newest messages. Use whatever technology your preferred email program offers. In Gmail, that'll be to tag all the messages with a new label called something like 'Hold', and archive them to get them out sight. In other programs, there will be folders or other methods.

THESE PREPARATIONS MAY take you a while, particularly if you need a couple of weeks' data from the first step. But once you've accomplished them, you're ready to carry out your escape.

How to execute your escape from email jail

STARTUP FOUNDERS OFTEN find that dealing with email takes up too much of their time — and that this can have profound effects on how well they run their companies. The previous chapter described how to tell whether email is the root of a wider problem, and how to prepare for a solution.

But preparation is only half the task. You may have your file ready to cut through the bars of your cell, and your sheets knotted for climbing down the prison walls. Now you actually have to execute your escape.

RASPID: Understand your options

First, pause for a moment to reflect how people get into email jail to begin with. Mostly, it's because they sit down to do some email, and then open a message that is not just an email, but a trigger for a task taking half an hour or an hour — which they get stuck into right away. An hour later, the task is complete. But they still have forty unanswered messages — plus another half-dozen that arrived in the meantime. Do that every day for three months, and you end up with 11,000 random messages in your inbox.

The solution is to have a clear algorithm for dealing with email. What I've seen the most successful CEOs do is this. When an email comes in, they choose between four options:

1. *Respond* to it immediately, but only if you can do so in two minutes or less.

2. *Acknowledge* it, *and Schedule* a time to deal with it. This is what you do when an email is really a trigger for a task that's too long to complete during your email session. If it's an hour-long task, it goes in the calendar; if it's just three minutes, then it goes on your to-do list (see page 246). But simply telling the other person that you've got it is much more important than it looks. To see why, reflect on your own irritation if you email someone and five days later have no idea whether they got your message or not. You're much happier if the recipient (a) confirms they got your message, (b) tells you what they're going to do about it, and (c) promises to deliver by a deadline. When the boot is on the other foot and you're the respondent, you can get the same kudos by simply remembering that the AS is a two-step: *Acknowledge* and *Schedule*, and making sure that your acknowledgement tells them when you're going to respond by.

3. Often people take on tasks they shouldn't do, simply because someone has asked them. That's why it's valuable to look at a request that's come in by email, and to ask the question Am I the person who should deal with this? If not, don't just do it anyway. Instead, pass on the request to the right person in your organisation — but again, tell the sender

what you're doing. In short, *Pass on* and *Inform*, or PI. Why inform? To avoid the annoying situation, which again you've probably experienced yourself, of getting no reply to a request, and then being told that the person who received your email delegated it to someone else — who was supposed to reply to you but didn't. That's why the second step is so important. The ideal PI also includes the direct contact details of the person to whom it's been passed on, and a message showing that you're still taking responsibility, like *Please get back to me in a week if Salim hasn't responded*. When appropriate, you can cc: in the delegate so both steps could be accomplished in a single message.

4.   *Decline*. Most people get requests for help that they're not going to fulfil, and many of them think it's OK just to ignore them. I'm a big fan of Adam Grant, who wrote a witty piece in the *New York Times* entitled "No, you can't ignore email; it's rude." Although it may seem harder to say no than pretend you never received the request, actually it's kinder. And it will sweeten the pill if you can explain in a friendly way why you can't or won't help (the snippets and canned messages I mentioned in my article on preparation do this in a couple of keystrokes). Grant agrees that there are a few types of email — for example obvious spam or rudeness — which you can ignore. Automated drip campaigns are an interesting grey area: they don't merit a personal response, since they're only fake-personal. But I decline rather than ignore for selfish reasons: to avoid the cognitive load of having to deal with the inevitable four automated follow-ups.

To remember the four options, you can write the acronym RASPID — Respond, Acknowledge-and-Schedule, Pass-on-and-Inform, Decline — on a card, and keep it near you ready for your first new email session. Those are your choices when faced with each new inbound email.

You'll need a system for where and how to keep track of the tasks you schedule and the things you have delegated. I use stars and labels in email; you'll be able to figure out what works for you. But whatever you choose, you'll need to follow it consistently. Here are some things that can help.

Measure your first session

The first time you deal with email using these new techniques, you'll be ready to breathe the fresh air outside the jail. Note the time you start dealing with your mail, and note how many unanswered emails there are in your inbox. (The previous chapter showed you what to do with the unanswered messages that have been accumulating for the past six months.) Then go through the messages, and check the time when you're done. You'll use this information to figure out how long it takes you on average to deal with email, and you can use this later on. You're done with your email either when you've finished up the allotted time slot, or when you've dealt with the newest email that was there when you started.

Start from the oldest, and don't scan

If you took the advice to switched off previews in your email, each message will be completely new to you. Since you've also set your email to progress from older to newer, you'll simply start from the oldest and keep going until you're up to date. For each message, use RASPID to decide, rapidly, what to do.

Resist 'inbox zero'

During the first session when you deal with email in this new way, new emails will probably come in while you're working, including some from people replying to your response. But it's not your mission to clear them now, since this target would require you to keep checking your mail after every task, every meeting, every phone call, to ensure that your inbox is clean, empty and polished. That gives a sense of satisfaction, but it's fake satisfaction — and achieving it will reduce your attention span to that of a gnat. Dealing with messages that arrive during the session will turn your inbox into a chat app, where the intervals between messages will shorten until you're batting messages back and forth every thirty seconds. Nobody ever built a billion-dollar business by keeping their inbox at zero. Rather, a good target is to aim for is a mean response time of a few hours, and a maximum response time of one working day. Think of the latter as your SLA with yourself.

Vacations and autoresponders

Once you know how many emails you can deal with in an hour, you can count the unread messages in your inbox after your vacation, and forecast how long it will take to deal with them.

If you're very lucky like me, then you can do something extreme: set an autoresponder which doesn't promise to deal with emails on your return, but tells people, in the friendliest possible way, that you're going to simply discard all email that arrived during your vacation, on the grounds that it probably no longer needs a reply, and that if they want one, you'd like them to set a diary note for the date of your return and resend their message then.

You have no idea how liberating that is. However, it tends to get a poor reaction from anyone who thinks they're *entitled* to your response. So it's not a smart career move if you're in sales, or if you have clients, or a boss who's not Danish. (A New York fund manager I met told me he was astounded when he moved to Copenhagen to learn that the entire firm shut down for three weeks in July; nobody did any work of any kind, even answering email.) But no matter how tightly you're chained to the hamster wheel, it's worth reflecting on the implications of this, and ensuring that when you take some time off, you block out enough time after your return to catch up on your backlog.

Mobile devices

Many people now use smartphones as their primary, or only, computing device. That brings benefits (if you've got a five-minute delay before a meeting, you can quickly knock off some emails), but also temptations. The biggest temptation is to scan — to look at the email but not reply, which means you'll end up with a load of messages that look half-familiar. Let this escalate, and you'll find your're reading each message three times before you reply. I'm 100% supportive of the idea of doing email on a phone if you can answer yes to these three questions:

- Can you compose messages as fast on your phone as on a

computer? Note that dictating isn't cheating, it's an acceptable strategy. If not — maybe because you're a 100-words-a-minute typist like me and many former journalists — stick to a computer or tablet.

• Do you have all the productivity tweaks described above available on your phone? If not, you'll be manually typing canned paragraphs on your phone that you could insert on a computer in a click or two.

• Can you resist the temptation to scan? If not, save your email for your computer, and use the free time that you're on your phone doing something you really love — like reading a great novel.

How to know when to give up

TWELVE YEARS AGO, I went to fundraise for a new startup from a guy who's a successful and effective operator in the European technology business. The meeting was a perfect illustration of the saying

> If you want advice, ask for money; if you want money, ask for advice.

I asked him to invest, and he explained in brutal detail why he wouldn't invest and why he thought the business wouldn't succeed.

That was the advice; I didn't take it. His reaction was based on half an hour's thought. I'd done probably one hundred hours of research on the issues we were discussing, and I thought I knew better than he did. So, ignoring his advice, I went ahead and raised a bit over a million, and started the business. And every time I met him over the next 18 months, he'd ask me the same question: "Are you still flogging that dead horse?"

I didn't admit that the horse was dead until eighteen months later, when I finally gave up and sent out the email to my investors apologising for having failed, explaining what

I thought had gone wrong, and letting them know that I'd be returning the chunk of their money that was left.

Animal-rights activists wouldn't like that dead-horse metaphor. The implication behind it is that it's OK to beat an animal if you want it to work harder, because the fear of pain will make it put in more effort — but there's no point flogging a horse that can't feel any pain, and therefore it won't be influenced no matter how viciously you hit it. I'd normally hesitate to revive the metaphor, except that in the startup space these days it's common to talk about 'crushing it' and 'killing it' as if companies (customers, or markets) were small animals, and torturing them to death is morally just fine.

But the metaphor of flogging a dead horse is a valuable one, because running startups is really hard. Founders put themselves through enormous effort and stress in an attempt to make their companies succeed, even though most founders could make twice the money for half the effort by taking a job in an established business. So it's hugely valuable to know whether all the effort is being wasted because the company is dead anyway, or whether it's worth continuing to crack the whip in the hope that just a little more effort might get you past the finishing line.

So how do you tell? How do you know whether the horse you're flogging is dead or alive?

THE STANDARD WAY of looking at this is quantitative, and the absolutely simplest approach is to consider the question of when you're likely to run out of money. To do this, compare the cash you have in the bank against your burn rate and growth rate, and work out what will happen if your expenses stay constant and your revenue continues to grow at the rate it's been growing over the past few months. Paul Graham, founder of YCombinator, wrote an insightful blog post in 2015 pointing out that you're 'default alive' if the growth rate is high enough that your revenues will exceed your expenses before you run out of cash. If not, you're 'default dead'.

It's possible to be default dead and yet still to have a good business. That's because companies often take a while to figure out who to sell their product to and how to reach potential customers cost-effectively, and move them through the sales cycle efficiently to the point where they start paying money. A quantitative way to capture this is the 'Bessemer CAC ratio', named from the venture firm that first came up with this analysis.

There's lots of complexity and subtlety to applying it in practice, but the one-liner is to look closely at the ratio between the lifetime value from a customer (LTV comes from multiplying the number of months a client will stay with you by the monthly gross margin or contribution margin, not the top-line revenue) and what the customer acquisition cost is. (CAC has to include all the marginal costs of bringing in that new customer: not just your ads, for instance, but also the person who manages them; not just the sales team but also the onboarding team.) If these unit economics are attractive, that's a signal to start spending a lot on sales and marketing, which results in high growth — at which point the company's attractive prospects become visible to all, and it's easy to raise funding.

But if you've made recent changes to your product, then your future client churn may be lower than it was in the past, which will increase your LTV. And if you've made recent changes to your sales and marketing, then the newest cohort of customers you've acquired may have cost a lot less than the early ones where you were experimenting and trying to figure out the best way to bring them in. So a straightforward CAC-ratio calculation may give you a more pessimistic answer than you think is fair: on a historic view, the business isn't good, but if you take only the last quarter or the last month, it may be fine. (You also need to consider the future, but aim off for your own optimism: most founders believe their future customers will stay loyal for longer than today's customers, and that their marketing will be more effective in future than in the past, but sadly most founders are wrong. Only detailed analysis and discussion can help you figure out whether your assumptions are well-grounded.)

You might think these are problems only for very early-stage companies, and I certainly see them often in the seed-stage investments we make at Walking Ventures. But I also see these questions at later on, where my relationship with the company is only as the CEO's coach. In many Series A companies, and a few Series B companies, sales still aren't growing on plan, and customers are still scarily expensive to acquire.

Yet even if there are concerns, venture capitalists find it hard to take the initiative and raise the alarm for their existing investments. Inbound deal flow comes from referrals, and telling a founder that their business is no good is like telling them their baby is ugly: it doesn't win you friends. Seasoned

VCs understand option value: a 20% stake in a business with a 10% chance of being worth $100m is worth more than shutting down a company early and salvaging $1m in cash from the wreckage. And there's also a shadier consideration: newer firms that are trying to raise a new fund will often prefer unsuccessful companies to stagger along discreetly in zombie status than to become an unequivocal fail that has to be reported to potential new investors in the VC's next fund.

So right up to Series B, there's a need to capture not just raw numbers but also some of the qualitative data on how things are going in order to figure out whether the business is likely to succeed, and whether it justifies more funding. I'd suggest the best way to do this is by considering five statements and deciding how strongly you agree with them.

1. *We've launched a product delivering real value that customers should pay for today.* You might think that's a long-winded way of saying 'we've launched an MVP', but here's the difference. A minimum viable product can be something that you don't actually expect clients to pay for. One reason might be that you need network effects, and the product can't be valuable to its first few users. But there can be other reasons too. The key question is whether you believe your product ought to be bringing in revenue right now. For your very first round of investment, you won't need to agree with the statement. But the more money you've raised and the longer you've been running, the more firmly you should agree.

2. *We've reached out and offered our product to an*

appropriate number of those potential customers. It's one thing to have built a good product; it's another thing to start marketing and selling it. To agree strongly with statement #2, you have to have both built a sales and marketing process and run it for long enough to get enough customers in at the top of the funnel. How many customers should you have approached? Obviously that depends on your target clients; if you're targeting whales who will pay $1m a year once the product is right, you'll need a hell of a lot fewer of them than if you're targeting $1,000-a-year rabbits, as German VC Christoph Janz calls them. But if you have a $10,000-a-year product that you believe is sellable and you've only gone out to ten clients, then you've got work to do.

3. *An appropriate proportion of potential customers have bought our product.* Until you've reached out to enough clients, your answer to whether you've correctly identified your target customer personas and figured out what problems they have and how to position your product to meet those problems is likely to be 'don't know'. But once you've got enough numbers in your funnel, you can start to tell from the stage-progression rates — the percentage of clients you emailed who replied, or the percentage of respondents who agreed to set up a demo, or the percentage of demos who started a trial, or whatever — how much your product looks to them like a solution to their problem. This is quite separate from whether the product *does* actually solve their problem. When customers say they 'don't have budget', what they mean is that they don't have budget for you: that is, they may have

a pile of money to spend on things, but your product doesn't look like a high enough priority to earn a place on the list.

4. *Customers who've paid for our product are using it appropriately frequently.* Obviously what counts as appropriate depends on your product. Larry Page of Alphabet uses the 'toothbrush test' as an investment criterion: do customers use the product once or twice a day, and does it make their life better? Yet on this test, Uber is close-but-no-cigar, and AirBnB is nowhere. So there are plenty of great companies that don't have a habit-forming frequency of usage — and in defining 'appropriate', you have to bear in mind your target customer persona. If your product is online consumer banking, you want to see people making it their primary account; if it's a tool to manage corporate marketing, people should be checking in daily. If it's a CRM, probably several times a day; if it's an at-home massage service, you want them to use it for most of their massages, so that may mean monthly or fortnightly. If customers aren't hitting your target frequency, that means either you've targeted the wrong clients or the product isn't right. Viral recommendation is also an indicator: if people aren't telling their friends about the product, that's a bad sign — unless your product provides a competitive advantage they'll want to keep secret, or it's something they may not want to shout to the world about, like a sex toy. You can still have a good business if this is the case, but you won't acquire customers for free.

5. *Our progress as measured by the statements above compares reasonably with our initial plan.* When you first

launch a business, there are lots of unknowns. And it's often easier to raise the first money from investors before you've launched, because their response will be more about what they think about the product and the team than about the hard evidence of what customers think about the product and whether those customers buy it. But it's still valuable to look back at your past plans, and ask tough questions about how you delivered on those plans. Most startups are too optimistic. Don't blame yourself for that: since the probability-adjusted value of starting a new business is usually less than staying in your day job, VCs would have very little to invest in if most startup founders and CEOs were truly rational. But your optimism has to be rationally bounded. If you've raised money two or three times, and each time given convincing reasons for why the business hadn't taken off yet but promised it would take off once the new money was in, then you won't be able to agree with statement #5. And you also need to pay attention to how long you've been going: if you're at a much earlier stage, and only expected to have got one or two pilot customers by now, then even if you're not agreeing strongly with statements #2 to #4, you may still be on track.

To decide the fate of your startup, ask the different stakeholders in the company to look at the five statements and evaluate each one by saying whether they strongly agree with it (score 5), agree (score 4), don't know or are on the fence (score 3), disagree (score 2), or strongly disagree (score 1).

Then average their results for each question. So for an example company, the average response might be 4.5 across all respondents to the product statement, 2.5 to the marketing statement (say because you've neglected it), 4 to the conversion statement because once you reach out to people they do actually buy, 3 to the usage statement and 2 to the progress-versus-plan statement.

Finally, multiply the average scores for each statement together. So the score for the example company above will be =4.5*2.5*4*3*2, which is 270.

Expectations of where you should be differ according to how much money you've raised, and how long you've been going for — and that's why the word 'appropriate' is so important in the statements. But a good rule of thumb could be as follows. If your combined score is more than 1,500, then your horse isn't just alive, it's a thoroughbred. The business has great prospects, and you're likely to be spoiled for choice when you raise money. If your score is over 750, then the business is very healthy. At a score of 500, you're in the middle of the startup pack, and so you should expect your chance of survival to be about average for the stage you're at. Below a score of 250, you need to ask serious questions about the health of your horse. And below 100, things will have to change fast if you're going to survive.

If you find it hard to decide how much you agree with the statements, that's understandable; industries differ, and products differ, so there's no quantitative test that works for all startups. But it's important to remember this: company founders and CEOs — even those who are serial entrepreneurs who've done it a couple of times before — usually have only a small data set to compare with. Investors who have dozens of portfolio companies and see thousands of companies a year are in a much better position to judge your company relative to the rest of the investable startup universe. That's why it's valuable to bring them into the discussion. But you need to do it in a way that encourages them not to tell you what they think you want to hear, but to give you honest answers.

If your investors aren't hugely value-adding, or you mistrust their judgment, then you may find it helpful to discuss the statements with an advisor, an investment banker, or a coach with investing and operating experience. But if none of those are possible, then you can always fall back on the most reliable, albeit time-consuming and painful, source of honesty: investors you pitch, in large numbers, for funding. Don't pay any attention to what they say: the answer that 'it's too early, but come and see us again in six months' is French for 'no'. Instead, pay attention to what new investors *do* when you reach out to them. Only the rarest and most confident investors will dare to give you an honest answer as to whether you're flogging a dead horse.

TIME
MANAGEMENT

How to keep a good to-do list

SINCE 1996, I'VE been thinking about the issue of how to put my working time to best use. It was when I switched from a career as a journalist at *The Economist* and the *Financial Times* to founding a startup — and then, post-NASDAQ, becoming a venture capitalist and then a CEO coach. Investing and company-building are very different beasts from journalism and other jobs in mature businesses. They need you to keep track of more things, and to take more initiatives. Being well-organised matters more.

One of the two most important things I've learned about using work time well is Stephen Covey's 'big rocks' analogy (see "How to actually complete your OKRs once they're set" on page 107). That's why I schedule two hours in my calendar every day for my One Big Thing.

The second important thing I learned comes from Dave Allen's book *Getting Things Done*. Most people have trouble with writing to-do lists, but don't realise why. It's because they've got items on the list that are impossible to do in one sitting. 'Organize vacation', for instance, isn't one task, it's a project made up of many tasks.

- Research possible destinations;
- Pick one;

- Decide on a way to get there, a place to stay and things to do
- Make bookings.

Allen tells you that those four things are 'next actions' — achievable in one session if done in the right order. But the project of 'Organize vacation' isn't doable as a stand-alone action, so it will only cause you frustration if you allow it on your to-do list.

Once you've given priority to the big rocks and broken out projects into next actions, though, you still need a way to keep track of them. Dave Allen noticed that to-do lists often included a confusing set of things that were irrelevant because you couldn't actually do them right now. You needed access to your office filing cabinet, or you needed your home phone, or your computer — so he came up with the idea of creating a separate list for each location. That's now out of date. Many startup founders and VCs today run their work mostly from a phone and can do almost any category of task any place, any time.

But just because you can do anything anywhere doesn't mean you should. If you have five minutes before your next meeting, there's little point starting something that needs fifteen minutes. So it's good to keep lists of quick tasks separate from things that need more thought or concentration.

And there's also value in 'habit stacking' — doing several similar things one after another, rather than incurring the switching cost of jumbling up random types of tasks together (see page 252). I like to schedule phone calls in blocks of an hour at a time, rather than allowing random inbound calls to interrupt my train of thought.

I've tried keeping to-do lists on spreadsheets, web apps, and mobile apps. And I've concluded that one of the most important things you can do with a to-do list is to *remove* things from it. Something that felt important last Tuesday may not be relevant today. Something you were going to apply for earlier this month has passed its deadline, and the only effect of seeing it on your to-do list is to feel worthless and guilty. That's one of the reasons I've switched back to low-tech: I've evolved a handwritten, paper to-do list, done on a template.

Here's the rhythm I've adopted: I end each working day by taking a fresh sheet printed with my template, and spend ten minutes writing my to-do list for tomorrow. While I'm at it, I write two things at the end of today's list that reflect on what has passed. If you're feeling that this use of paper seems profligate in the days of climate change, no worries: you can print template to-do lists on the back of junk mail or other stuff you can feed into your printer.

There's another small benefit of producing a to-do list with a pen each day: you can view updating the list as an opportunity for a little calligraphy practice — which can make your handwriting more beautiful.

Rather than scrunch up my completed to-do list into a ball and throwing it away at the end of each day, I add it to a neat pile of sheets that provide an interesting record of what got done and didn't get done over recent weeks, months, and eventually years.

So what are the ingredients of the perfect to-do list

template? From the template that I've iterated over the past few years, I'd say there are six. I've shared them with a number of the CEOs I coach, and some of them have found this approach transformative.

1. *A reminder of the wider objectives I'm trying to achieve.* This can be projects, or OKRs. But the important thing is that every time I look at my to-do list, I run the risk of getting bogged down in detail. To start by focusing on the high level, it's good to see that first — right at the top of the list. Writing it each evening at the top of my to-do list creates a little pressure to ensure that the tasks I write tonight for tomorrow are connected with my wider objectives.

2. *A note of the One Big Thing (OBT) to achieve today.* It's easy to be side-tracked into doing things that are urgent but not important, and that's why it's so valuable to block out time in the calendar to think and work on something serious. But it's hard to sit down in front of an empty screen and simply dream up something on the spur of the moment that justifies a couple of hours of focused energy. If I have that 'OBT' already chosen last night and written on today's to-do list, it's much easier to jump right in.

When I don't get to complete the OBT, I'm going to have some work left over. There's space beneath my one big thing to record those leftovers so they actually get finished, and that's also a good place to record less important but still unfinished tasks.

3. *Big jobs, small jobs, phone calls, and so on, broken out into separate mini-lists.* Those mini-lists make it easy to find exactly what can best fill five minutes while waiting for an Uber, or which task to pick if I'm feeling low in energy and have fifteen minutes before a conference call. If I'm walking to a meeting, then it's helpful to have a list of people to call. Five minutes, 15 minutes, and calls are therefore my categories; there may be others specific to you.

4. *Space for scratch notes.* Since I've got a paper to-do list, which gives the satisfaction of crossing items off as they're done, I can use it as a scratch pad for notes, too. So there's a little space for recording details that I want to save during the day.

5. *A record of three things achieved during the day.* Many of us who have lots of things to do can easily fall into the trap of looking at what remains undone at the end of the day — so many things reproaching us, and so few days when we actually got to the end of the list — that it's no wonder we feel depressed. In fact, our achievements are there, but they're in negative space, noticeable only by their absence because we checked them off. (In my paper to-do list, things done today are neatly crossed through so I can see them: much more satisfying than seeing them disappear.) But it's still valuable to have a positive list of achievements.

So at the end of each day, I like to write down three things that got done. Some days, the three things will be impressive; on other days, they'll be so tiny that I'd be ashamed to show them to anyone. No matter: recording those three things at the end of each day, big or small, gives me a sense of accomplishment.

6. *A mini gratitude diary.* There's lots of empirical evidence that noticing the good things in our lives, and keeping track of them, is good for our mental and physical health. At the end of each day, I write down three things that I'm grateful for.

SO THOSE ARE the ingredients of my template paper to-do list. The rhythm works like this.
- At the end of each working day, write tomorrow's list.
- Then finish off today's list by writing the three achievements and the three reasons for being grateful.
- Add today's list to your pile of completed lists.
- Tomorrow morning, start the day by looking at the list.
- Cross out each thing as it gets done.
- Rinse and repeat.

How batching and stacking can fix your time management

THERE WAS A time when I was a CEO — I think while our company was growing from 25 to 50 people in the space of seven months — when I began to feel overwhelmed. It wasn't just the ever-broadening range of things I was expected to do. It wasn't just the queue of people that formed by my desk wanting to discuss stuff or check something. It wasn't just the to-do lists that kept getting longer. No: the real killer was the 'multi-tasking' — the way that I'd often have to interrupt what I was doing in order to do something else, and then I'd get interrupted while doing that something else, until it got to the point where I couldn't even remember what I was trying to do to begin with.

Note that I've wrapped the word 'multi-tasking' in quotation marks. As I've said, human beings aren't truly capable of paying attention to two things at once. We're more like single-core microprocessors, where we create the appearance of that by switching rapidly back and forth between them. But that switching has an overhead with people, just like it does with processors: lower efficiency, worse performance, and sometimes breakdown.

While this was happening to me at work, I knew there had to be a better way. But it took me a number of years to find it.

THE JOURNEY STARTED when I was reading the brilliant book *Sum: Forty Tales of the Afterlife* by David Eagleman, a Stanford neuroscientist, which proposes forty possibilities, in the form of stories, for what might happen to us after we die. The first one he calls 'Sum', and it goes like this:

> In the afterlife you relive all your experiences, but this time with the events reshuffled into a new order: all the moments that share a quality are grouped together.

So imagine the implications of that:

> You spend two months driving the street in front of your house, seven months having sex. You sleep for thirty years without opening your eyes. For five months straight you flip through magazines while sitting on a toilet. You take all your pain at once, all twenty-seven intense hours of it. Bones break, cars crash, skin is cut, babies are born. Once you make it through, it's agony-free for the rest of your afterlife.

Sound good? Wait; there are drawbacks:

> One minute realizing your body is falling. Seventy-seven hours of confusion. One hour realizing you've forgotten someone's name. Three weeks realizing you are wrong. Two days lying. Six weeks waiting for a green light. Seven hours vomiting. Fourteen minutes experiencing pure joy. Three months doing laundry. Fifteen hours writing your signature. Two days tying shoelaces.

If you took things that far, Eagleman admits, the result wouldn't be pleasant. You'd probably look back with nostalgia on your imperfect, disordered life on earth, and wish you could go back to it: "a life where episodes are split into tiny swallowable pieces, where moments do not endure, where one experiences the joy of jumping from one event to the next like a child hopping from spot to spot on the burning sand."

So there are limits to how much order you might want to bring to your life. A good way to check those limits can be seen in a great book called *The Art of Cleanup* by Swiss comedian Ursus Wehrli. Here's a guy who really puts things in their proper places. Straight-line pretzels. French fries taken out of their carton and lined up neatly to be counted. Alphabet soup neatly sorted into letter order. Colour-coded washing. Public-transport signs with the station names in one place and the lines neatly in another.

That might be going too far. But I realised I needed astart.

Learning from President Obama's suits

When Michael Lewis interviewed Barack Obama for *Vanity Fair*, he learned something useful about dress choices. "You'll see I wear only gray or blue suits," the president said. "I'm trying to pare down decisions. I don't want to make decisions about what I'm eating or wearing. Because I have too many other decisions to make."

If you're a startup CEO, your days aren't going to be boring. They'll be a mixture of reactive and proactive stuff. They'll be full of different activities. They're also probably full of surprises. So with all this variety in the *content* of your day, you don't need to create variety in its *structure*. You don't need to spend lots of time thinking about when, where and how long your meetings will be.

That's why it can be valuable to block out times of the day and week when you're doing activities that are unique, but are all of similar type. So my first step, once I started working as a VC, was to move the bulk of my first meetings with entrepreneurs to the same time and place every day: a couple of one-hour walking meetings, starting at 8am or 9am at a statue in the park. This helped me get those things done before the rest of the day starts, and had the extra benefit of not requiring manual scheduling: rather than having six emails fly back and forth for each appointment, I used a calendar tool to share a link with people allowing them to choose the time and day most convenient for them. (It's true that this puts thirty seconds' burden on them, but most people feel that's a small price to pay for a great deal more flexibility in choosing a date.)

I also started standardising and batching other types of meetings: four half-hour videocalls batched up into a single two-hour slot in the day, and four fifteen-minute phone calls batched up into a different hour in the day. (These leave more time for deep work, but need to be handled with care: that means setting the batches at different times on different days of the week, to be respectful of how other people order their days.)

When you start noticing batching, you see it everywhere. Take restaurants: at the fast-casual Asian noodle chain Wagamama, the chefs cook everything fresh to order, but not by one by one. They'll dish up two chicken katsu curries at a time or three miso-glazed cod ramen at a time. That has a small drawback for customers: instead of arriving at the same time for everyone, the food will appear randomly. But since it's probably only 1.2 times as much work to make three cod ramens instead of one, everyone benefits from the saving of effort — and since the restaurants are busy, the wait time is short.

Learning from open-heart surgery

Batching is a great way you can reduce the stress and overhead of having to keep track of lots of identical things at once. But what do you do when the things aren't identical? Here there's a useful insight from Atul Gawande, a top surgeon in Boston who also covers health policy for the *New Yorker*. In his brilliant book *The Checklist Manifesto*, Gawande reveals how even the most experienced and talented doctors can make mistakes, particularly when they're doing something complex with lots of steps and lots of concentration. Surgeons sew up patients with sponges, pens and even scalpels inside them.

What Gawande learned was that a simple step-by-step checklist can help eliminate these errors. Airline pilots have used them for years; unfortunately, doctors haven't, and many of them declared themselves insulted by even the suggestion that they might make a mistake. Hence the need for Gawande's book. He has had to struggle to persuade senior doctors that they're not infallible. As a result of Gawande's work, a number of hospitals persuaded their most talented people that following a checklist isn't an insult to their intelligence — and the result is a higher success rate in the operating room and lower infections in the ward.

I applied this in my own work by identifying the many small tasks that need to be done regularly, and turning them into checklists that can be easily followed. The items don't have to be related, or part of a sequence that makes up a bigger whole. But there's a benefit in doing them together, because that allows you to knock off a stack of small tasks in one go — and once you do this regularly, you've got a 'habit stack'.

SJ Scott's book *Habit Stacking* gives some valuable advice on how to create habit stacks. Pick a number of things that take less than five minutes each, that aren't part of some bigger whole, and that are simple to complete and improve your life or your work. Put them in a logical order and create a checklist for them that takes 30 minutes or less to complete. And then do them every day or every week as required.

To make habit stacks work.

• Choose an appropriate time and location for them so that you can regularly get them done.

• Build one routine at a time, rather than trying to check-listify your entire life in one go. Start with small, satisfying wins.

• Make yourself accountable by telling someone else about the new process you've put in, and asking them to check with you how it's going.

• Do your best to repeat regularly on the schedule you've decided, and finally give yourself some rewards, even if they're small, for succeeding.

BATCHING AND STACKING may not sound life-changing or exciting. But when I started using them to manage my time and my projects, the result was clear: I got more done. I was able to concentrate better. I was less stressed in the evenings and on weekends, and had less worry and doubt about things I might have forgotten to do.

How to save your marriage
from your startup

IT TOOK A question from my three-year-old son one morning at breakfast to make me realise how much harm my startup was doing to my marriage. The night before, I'd come home late from work (as usual), tired (as usual), stressed (as usual), and in a filthy mood. And I had been unkind to my wife.

For the past two years, as I'd been building a startup and driving it towards an IPO, she'd been a model of calm, patience and kindness. But when my behaviour finally crossed a line, she wasn't left with many options. I was in the kitchen, being nasty about something, and stepped outside to a closed-in patio to smoke (yes, the need to do that was a symptom too). So she locked me out. Then she opened a window, looked me in the eye, and said, "You can come back in when you're ready to be reasonable."

But I was angrier than ever, and took it out on the nearest thing: a group of plants in pots that we'd nurtured together into a tiny but beautiful jungle. I picked up a pot, dropped it on the tiles, and watched her reaction as it shattered into shards, spreading earth everywhere. Then I picked up another, and broke that too. Then a third, and a fourth.

I can't remember what finally brought me back to sanity. But I do remember my three-year-old noticing the piles of compost and the shards of terracotta outside the kitchen window the next morning and trying to figure out how they got like that. When his mother explained that I'd broken them, he looked at me. "Why do you break pots, Daddy?"

It's a truism to say that we all want to have happy lives, and that if we're in long-term relationships then we want those relationships to also be happy. That's probably the most common pair of goals among adults on the planet. Yet we can easily get into situations at work that begin to corrode our lives at home, and work pressures can end up destroying relationships. This is particularly true among startup founders, because fast-growing companies in bull markets offer the tantalising vision of an exit so valuable that for the rest of your life, you'll be free to decide what work you want to do (if any). So there's a temptation to say that you have no choice. You do what you have to do at work, if you want the prize, and put up with the side-effects on your relationship.

That's one common, extreme, response to the problem. The other extreme is to say that you need to give it all up: you'll be happier, according to this line of argument, if you abandon the ambition that prompted you to start the business in the first place.

Consider: a billionaire goes to a tropical island on vacation, and spends every day with a fisherman, out at sea. At the end of the week, he thanks the fisherman, gives him a $500 tip, and offers him a piece of free business advice. "Why don't you start a company, hire another boat, and pay someone to pilot it?" he asks. "In this resort alone, you could run twenty boats, and there's ten more resorts within an hour's sailing. You could turn this into a $100m business."

"And what would I do then?" asks the fisherman.

"Sell the business and retire," replies the billionaire. "You'd be free to spend all your time fishing."

"I am already." says the fisherman.

THIS DILEMMA IS more common than you might think. Although the caricature we have of startup founders is that they're all white, male, single, and 25, the average startup founder is considerably older. Many have partners, spouses and children. During the summer I was writing this book, among the startup founder-CEOs that I coach, two got married; one had a baby; and one divorced. It's not limited to startups or to CEOs either: plenty of the VCs I know, and a good number of people in high-powered jobs in government or not-for-profits as well as in business, face the same challenge.

Fixing the mistaken assumption

Start by recognising that the root of the problem is an assumption: the idea that it's all-or-nothing, that you have to sacrifice either your relationship or your startup. Once you let go of that notion, you're at a different starting-point: you're recognising that your job is going to put pressure on your relationship, but you're now looking for ways to lighten that pressure and maintain your relationship.

That pressure has five sources. The route to a solution lies in identifying your sources of pressure, creating a plan to mitigate them, and then monitoring how the plan is going.

ASTIL: The five ways a startup can destroy a marriage

When you're overworked, you're different in a number of ways. Look at this checklist (with your partner or spouse), and see how many you recognise. Are you:

Absent? Before my pot-breaking incident, I was in the office until 9pm most weekdays, and at least one weekend day. Hours like these mean less time to do fun stuff with your partner or spouse; less time to do your fair share of household chores and less time for your kids if you have them. Your significant other won't find that fair. It puts more work on them to do two people's homemaking or parenting tasks.

Stressed? Lots of people have some stress at work, but this is about bringing the stress home. When running a startup, I certainly wasn't good at leaving my troubles at the office. It's easier than you might think to get into the habit of holding it together for your team (after all, if you're a CEO, it's your job) but then (like me) falling to pieces at home, and letting rip with behaviour that would shock your board members if they were around to see it.

Tired? Your partner can reasonably expect that after those long hours you've put in, the two of you can do fun stuff in the limited time that's left. But no. You're so wrecked from the physical and emotional effort of work that your favourite activity on the weekend is... sleeping, watching TV, gaming, or doing something undemanding and solitary. That's not fair. If their life plan was to hook up with an octagenarian, they'd be loitering around the nearest old-people's home.

Inattentive? It's bad enough that from your spouse's point of view, you're no longer the happy, loving, energetic, person they chose as their life partner. But it's worse than that. Now you're not even present. You take calls from the team or your investors all the time. You check your email the minute they go to the bathroom. And when you grudgingly, dutifully spend time with your kids in the park, your spouse gets a call from a stranger reporting that your four-year-old has been found wandering the streets. Meanwhile, you were absorbed in your phone.

Lonely? The four points above make up a reasonable list of things your partner could complain about you. Despite that, you still feel a bit sorry for yourself — you don't feel understood, you don't get enough moral support, you're alone. When asked how it's going, you've been heard to answer: "I'd rather not talk about it."

IF YOU'D ANSWER yes to two of these items on your checklist, or if your partner would answer yes to three, then you need to have a conversation. If you'd say yes to three, or they'd say yes to four, then you need to have a conversation *today*.

The relationship-saving conversation

The conversation begins by agreeing on the symptoms. The ground rules are that you'll avoid moral judgments, demands, denials of responsibility, comparisons or assuming that anyone deserves anything. You'll be frank about your needs and requests. And you'll promise to use the tools of non-violent communication: describing your observations, not your opinions; your feelings, not your evaluations.

Next, you can propose a set of actions to remedy the situation, and ask for your partner's suggestions and support.

To be less *absent*, you need to stop viewing time with your loved ones as traded off against the activities you do at the *end* of each day. Many CEOs find that the end of the day is the best time for thinking, planning, or getting deep work done free from interruptions — things that could be particularly damaging to sacrifice that time. Instead, if you'd like to come home from work an hour earlier, try to identify your *least* productive hour of the day (whatever time it takes place) and eliminate that instead. Improve your handling of email. Run your meetings more effectively: switch one-on-ones to group sessions, and meetings to lunches, breakfasts or walks. Hold people accountable for delivering on time. Replace micromanagement with coaching. Set realistic objectives and key results, and review them regularly. Be more honest about people who take up too much of your time because they were hiring mistakes. Improve your relationship with your board. Give more training. Change your team's culture to take more responsibility without you.

To be less *stressed*, first consider this: is the underlying issue you're bringing home simply the question of whether you're in the right job or not? If the objective is partly to maximise the value of your shareholding in your startup, then firing yourself or moving yourself aside may be worth considering. Once you confirm that you are in the right job, work on becoming more mindful about your behaviour at home.

Identify what you're really feeling about work (frustrated? fearful? angry? humiliated?) and tell your partner what those feelings are. Once you've identified the feelings to yourself, you'll find it easier to avoid being snappy or grumpy with your partner without knowing why. If your startup isn't doing well, have an open conversation about what would happen if it failed and you had to get another job. Given your talents, that's unlikely to be catastrophic. Consider meditation.

To be less *tired*, focus more on your work *habits* than your work *hours*. Are you on a screen at home before sleeping? Do you have an irregular bedtime? Then look at your broader life. Are you getting too few hours of sleep? Are you eating wrong, or not taking enough exercise? Are you using drugs (including alcohol, caffeine and tobacco) to deal with the pressure, which have the side-effect of making you more tired afterwards? If the answer to any of these questions is yes, then you'll need to acquire a new set of habits. Not an easy task, but one that is a load more achievable with your loved one's support than alone.

To be less *inattentive*, it's worth reflecting on why you're not paying attention. It could be worry: you have a nagging feeling that there's stuff you should have done or forgot to do, which gnaws at you while you're looking into your loved one's eyes or hearing about their day. If so, your issue is that you need to figure out your to-do list more effectively, so that when you down tools at the end of the week, you've certainly captured everything you that you need to be doing. Alternatively, the reason for your inattention might be that big stuff is happening in your startup. I remember when my company was raising a $50m funding round, and there were lots of calls with lawyers and investors: it made my family's normal life seem slow and tame. Here it's helpful to think deeply about that person that you love, and why you care about them. A bit of loving-kindness meditation may help; I'd recommend the writing of Vietnamese monk Thich Nhat Hanh.

To be less *lonely*, it can help to set aside the normal reasons you might give for not confiding in your partner. Don't worry that they "won't understand"; try them anyway. And remember that while you try to play the hero at work, you're allowed to be just a normal, weak, failing person at home. "Peu d'hommes ont esté admirés par leurs domestiques," as the French 16th-century philosopher Montaigne said — or as someone later paraphrased it, no man is a hero to his own valet. There's something hugely cathartic about telling someone you love all the reasons why you feel inadequate and miserable.

YOU DON'T HAVE to pick any, let alone all, of the potential actions above. But if you sit down with your spouse, acknowledge the need for change, and make a plan for it, then you'll be making a start. You can set a date for a follow-up conversation to see how things are going. And you're in with a chance — I won't say a certainty, but a chance — to switch your marriage or your relationship from something that suffers collateral damage from your startup problems to something that makes you more resilient and more able to deal with them.

How about me? Well, soon after the pot-breaking incident, I concluded that I should step down — and that's what I did, timed precisely to match my company's IPO. I wrote the S1 (the registration statement you file with the SEC to take a company public), and a newly hired CEO did the roadshow to public investors. But the world has moved on since then; you no longer need to choose between your relationship and your startup. And one of my greatest satisfactions as a coach these days is helping startup founders figure out the right balance between the two.

How to run a startup
in one day a week

"YOU'VE NO IDEA how stressful it is," said Thomas. "Before all this started, I was working eleven-hour days. Now I'm working most weekends as well, and I no longer feel rested on Monday. But I'm not keeping up. Stuff isn't getting done. If this continues for another month,the business will fall apart."

If you're a startup founder who has done a funding round, Thomas's experience may sound familiar. At the start, it may not seem that big a deal to meet a couple dozen investors, answer info requests from four or five, and negotiate with two or three to finally strike a deal with one of them. But closing a round, as one of the CEOs I coach put it, is "the mother of all time-sinks".

And if you're realistic about what's involved, you can see why. A reasonable forecast might be 10 hours to prepare the pitch, 10 hours to practise it, 50 hours to travel back and forth to 25 meetings, 20 hours to satisfy investors' due diligence needs, 15 hours on follow-up meetings, and 10 hours negotiating with the eventual investor. That's 140 hours altogether — more than three weeks of full-time work — and if it's harder or slower to raise than planned, then expect to double that.

As a result, I often advise startup CEOs I'm coaching to

think of fundraising as a job that takes up 80% of their time — the equivalent of four days a week. If you go into a fundraising process hoping that you can somehow carry on running your company as you did before, then you're likely to be faced with a choice of unappetising outcomes: either overwhelming stress and exhaustion, or serious neglect of the business which may itself harm the fundraising if investors notice.

MOST CEOS COME up with a couple of strategies to deal with this problem by themselves. One is to get outside help on the fundraising by hiring in contractors to put together the financials and the slide deck; another is to delegate work to a strong CFO, VP Sales and CTO. But often, more drastic intervention is needed.

1. *Halve the time required for your one-on-ones (OOOs).* If you don't already meet the people who report to you regularly and individually, you should consider doing so. It's a valuable way to empower them to take responsibility. But OOOs have a drawback; if you begin with a chat to warm up, then it can take a while for the conversation to focus on work issues.

During fundraising, you don't have that luxury: you're a 'wartime CEO', as Ben Horowitz would put it. So you can explain to your team that you're going to need to halve the time allocated to OOOs. You can ask everyone to write you an update beforehand — either sent by email or in a structured document. The result is that you can still listen to your team's concerns and give the same input and support, but can get to the heart of the issues much more quickly.

2. *Double the time you spend on all-hands or team meetings.* In companies of under 100 people, assembling all hands for a regular update from the CEO on what's going on — and perhaps an AMA, or 'ask me anything' — is a great way to make sure that people not only understand what the company is trying to achieve but also feel a sense of allegiance to its mission and feel that their ideas and concerns are being listened to.

But during fundraising, when you're likely to be less around and less visible, and when the team may be feeling more curious or anxious about the company's future than normal, it's more important than ever to do them. Many CEOs use online tools to help employees suggest questions and then upvote them, so you know what topics concern people most and can address them.

3. *Double your breakfasts, lunches, walks and runs with your team.* To stay healthy during the fundraising, you'll want to make sure you get enough sleep, enough healthy food, and enough exercise — yet the pressure can often keep you tied to your desk. Since you're going to be around less for your team, it can be valuable to use good habits to see more of them. Invite your management team to breakfast. Take new hires to lunch. If one of your reports likes keeping fit, hold a meeting with them over a walk or a jog. Obviously this isn't appropriate where you need to refer to documents or sit in front of a screen together — but when much of the benefit is about build-

ing relationships between people, or understanding personal issues, the displacement activity can actually help, rather than hinder, the conversation.

When they start tracking how they allocate their days (see below), many CEOs are astounded to learn how often they stop what they're doing to respond to unplanned questions and spontaneous requests from help or input from their team. The total amount of time may not seem problematic, but the frequency is: if you're trying to concentrate on a task, each interruption takes you away from what you were doing, and there's lots of psychological evidence that switching back and forth makes you less effective.

4. *Halve unnecessary or spontaneous requests for help.* Every 'one-liner' interruption you deal with, whether it's to sign off on wireframes for the product, to approve a fresh marketing hire to Salesforce, to make payments from the company bank account, may feel insignificant of itself. But ten of those a day could take an hour away from time you could have spent on fundraising. And even worse, each one will make it harder to return to whatever you were working on before.

That's why it's a great idea to warn people that because of the demands of fundraising, you're going to be less available for spontaneous questions and you'd like people to plan ahead by thinking of issues that might come up in the next week and raising them with you at your regular OOOs. This has two effects: it reduces your cognitive load, but it also puts a little pressure on people to think hard on what they might want to ask. This builds their independence. And when they seek advice, your first response can be to ask 'Well, what would you think makes most sense?' This change can help you become a better manager, because you're building independence among your reports and making decisions for them less often.

Thomas told me about all the decisions and questions he had to deal with day by day. But when pressed, he admitted that only a minority of those things truly needed him. This was in part because of habits he'd established when his company was still small, and in part because his reports had acquired the habit of asking his approval for even small things.

THOMAS SOLVED THE problem by making a list of all the processes for which his input was currently required, and reassigning them: some delegatable to others; some still requiring his input; and some where his reports would be able to handle it themselves with only a little training. "I was astounded," he said afterwards. "The time pressure during fundraising forced me to stop doing some of those things — and they gave me a permanent increase in my productivity afterwards as a result."

What forces you to reevaluate your role in operating the business could be something external like a fundraising, or something internal like a special project. Or it could simply be that you take the initiative to review — regularly — your responsibilities, and how you could devolve some of them to other people in your organisation.

But the effort is usually worth it. It can liberate a significant chunk of your time for work that is more valuable. And by giving your team more autonomy, it can increase their job satisfaction and their commitment.

Acknowledgements

GIVEN HOW MANY ideas we all absorb from the ether around us, I can't hope to thank all the founders and CEOs these lessons come from. But here's at least a partial list of people to whom I'm extremely grateful:

Aysha Ali, Rasim Aliyev, Leo Anthias, Elizabeth Apelles, Alice Bentinck, Adam Bird, Johan Brissmyr, Bernadine Broecker, Luca Cafici, Alastair Campbell, Jamie Carruthers, Charlie Casey, Jean-Michel Chalayer, Yoel Cheshin, Nicola Chilman, Matt Clifford, Oli Cummings, Nino d'Adhemar, Jakob Dahlberg, Pete Dowds, Kai Eberhardt, Nigel Eccles, Annika Erikson, Mark Evans, Alex Green, Olivier Grinda, Gaby Hersham, Dominic Hill, Eli Hoffman, Tim Holladay, Ben Iceton, Munir Jawed, Peter Kecskemethy, Freddy Kelly, Mindaugas Kriščiūnas, Fabio Kuhn, David Langer, Weiting Liu, Mark Locker, Srin Madipalli, Ben Maruthappu, Ivan Mazour, Luke McCormick, Mark McDermott, Matthias Metternich, Chris Mitchell, Melissa Morris, Oliver Muller, Philip Mundy, Andrew Newell, Pawel Nowak, Andrew O'Brien, Anna Ottosson, Richard Pither, William Reeve, Will Roberts, Sten Saar, Tim Sadler, Theo Saville, Jan-Erik Solem, Anna Tsyupko, Daniel van Binsbergen, Erwin Werring, Richard White and Tom Williams.

I've also learned a great deal from a number of insightful

investors and others in the startup ecosystem: Joel Ayala, Ben Blume, Harry Briggs, Ophelia Brown, Grace Cassy, Suranga Chandratillake, Toby Coppel, Alexander De Carvalho, Daniel Doll-Steinberg, David Dwek, Ian Forshew, Alan Foster, Alain Gavin, Dan Glazer, Frédéric Halley, Julia Hawkins, Paul Haydock, Ankur Jain, Mat Kaliski, Jon Lerner, Simon Levene, Luciana Lixandru, Cecilia Lundborg, Bruce Macfarlane, Jose Marin, Ivan Mazour, Stephen Millard, Ed Mitchinson, Simon Murdoch, James Penn, Sean Seton-Rogers, Denis Shafranik, Kiana Sharifi, Matthew Stafford, Tomasz Swieboda, Rokas Tamošiūnas, Shie-Haur Tan, Phil Wilkinson and Hana Yang.

And finally, I'd like to thank Sam at Corvid Content for highly skilled copy-editing, Daniel for insightful typographical advice, Emily for artistic imagination, and Michael and Judy for setting inspiring examples of how to write books and how to learn new things.

Printed in Great Britain
by Amazon